leading in english

HOW TO CONFIDENTLY COMMUNICATE AND INSPIRE OTHERS IN THE INTERNATIONAL WORKPLACE

D. Vincent Varallo
Joerg Schmitz
Stephan M. Mardyks

WILEY

Cover design: Wiley

Published by John Wiley & Sons, Inc., Hoboken, New Jersey.
Published simultaneously in Canada.

For general information about our other products and services, please contact our Customer
Care Department within the United States at (800) 762-2974, outside the United States
at (317) 572-3993 or fax (317) 572-4002.

Wiley publishes in a variety of print and electronic formats and by print-on-demand. Some
material included with standard print versions of this book may not be included in e-books
or in print-on-demand. If this book refers to media such as a CD or DVD that is not
included in the version you purchased, you may download this material at http://
booksupport.wiley.com. For more information about Wiley products, visit www.wiley.com.

ISBN: 9781119361305 (cloth); ISBN 9781119361329 (ePDF); ISBN 9781119361336 (ePub)

Printed in the United States of America

10 9 8 7 6 5 4 3 2 1

Contents

Acknowledgments

We would like to thank our wives, Ivette, Latha, and Marie-Genet, and our families for their support, patience, and enthusiasm for this project.

Our sincere gratitude goes to our dedicated team who played an instrumental role in guiding this book to publication:

- Christina Schmitz, who helped us organize our thoughts and sharpen our focus
- David Westley Covey, whose astute suggestions helped the manuscript flow
- Carmela O'Flaherty for her support and excellent contributions to the Toolkit
- Maggie Kennedy and Jacquelyn Hayward, whose expertise in manuscript submissions proved invaluable
- The team at Cape Cod Compositors for their proficient copyediting skills
- The team at Wiley for their ongoing support and for patiently guiding this book to publication
- David M. R. Covey, Ken Price, and our colleagues at Thomas-Leland for their ongoing support

We also would like to thank our clients worldwide and the many international professionals we have met along the way who have told us their stories and placed their trust and confidence in us.

Finally, we dedicate this book to the international professionals who are on a journey to find their authentic voice across cultural and linguistic backgrounds. We wish you the success you truly deserve.

At the Airport Lounge

Liz stood impatiently in front of the large screens outlining the departures and arrivals for the afternoon's travels. Her eyes fixed on departing flights, as the airline had yet to post her gate. She anxiously waited, her bag hanging heavily on her right shoulder, and her suitcase on the floor in front of her. The crowd around her got larger, she could hear a young child behind her crying to her mother for another piece of candy, but her gaze stayed fixed on the bright blue departure screen. After what felt like hours of waiting, the dreaded word "DELAYED" appeared next to her flight in big, bold, red letters.

Liz mumbled under her breath, "Another delay . . . great . . . ."

She grabbed her suitcase and begrudgingly decided to have a drink to get her through what was now a six-hour layover. Liz was very familiar with the Los Angeles International Airport (LAX). She made her way to her favorite lounge and took a seat at a small round table near the bar. She ordered a dirty martini and logged in to the WiFi to check her e-mail. She looked up to get the bartender's attention for a snack menu and noticed a man enter the lounge, seeming frustrated. He let his briefcase fall to the floor as he whipped off his jacket, folded it, and placed it neatly on a barstool. He took a seat at the bar and flipped through the menu. Liz was unable to get the bartender's attention as he made his way to attend to his new customer.

"What can I get for you, sir?" said the bartender to the man.

"I would like an am-buh-gah medium rare with cheese and a glass of waw-ta with gas please," said the man slowly in a strong French accent.

The bartender looked at the man and asked, "Can you say that again, buddy?"

The man repeated his order, but the bartender still looked perplexed as he tried to understand what exactly he needed to write down on his order pad. The man began getting more and more frustrated as he continually repeated himself. At this point he must have ordered eight or nine hamburgers and mineral waters! Liz overheard their struggle and offered her help.

"I think he would like a cheeseburger and a glass of water. If you have sparkling water that would be great," she said from her table and added, "and can I get the snack menu, please?"

Both of them looked in her direction. The look of confusion eased from the bartender's face as he breathed a sigh of relief and put the order in. The man looked over at Liz, still visibly frustrated, but offered up a friendly "Thanks."

"You're very welcome," Liz said. "I have the same problem where I live."

"Oh, really? Where are you from?"

"I am originally from New Jersey, but I was relocated to Brazil four months ago for work. I probably wouldn't have interrupted you when you were ordering, but when I'm in Brazil speaking English some people can't seem to understand my New Jersey accent. When I heard you ordering, it really hit home for me. I know how it feels."

The man's mouth widened into a smile. "That's pretty funny, because you speak great English, and it's your native language but people still can't understand your accent? I don't believe—"

"Even when I'm traveling throughout the United States people always say, 'You must be from New Joisey,'" Liz interrupted as she exaggerated her words to create the classic New Jersey accent. "Where are you from?" she asked the man.

"I am from France but I work for a Swedish manufacturing company in the UK."

Liz smiled. "I'm Liz, by the way," she said as she stuck her hand straight out for him to shake.

"I'm Pierre," he said as he stretched across an empty seat to meet her hand.

"So what brings you to the United States?" Liz questioned.

"I was doing a site visit for my company in Houston, and then I had a quick meeting in LA. Now I'm going back to headquarters in Stockholm. You know, with my heavy French accent people don't understand me easily. In business it's not too bad, but when I try to order things, like today, sometimes it is pretty difficult. It seems like a lot of people find me hard to understand."

Liz nodded her head in understanding. "What happens with me feels even more challenging because it's my native language, and I feel like an outsider when I'm speaking English in Brazil. I can really empathize with your situation."

Pierre's eyes widened and he shook his head in disbelief. He looked at Liz. "Unreal—you sound so clear. But truthfully, when I speak English with non-native English speakers—I mean, when I'm with my colleagues from Sweden, and Mexico, and Dubai—we don't have problems to work with and understand each other. In my mind, the major issue is when we work with native English speakers—our American, English, or even Australian colleagues. I feel that there is a bigger disconnect there. It should be a two-way street, but they make it seem like it is our problem . . . as if only the non-native English speakers have the problem. The truth is we have a hard time understanding them, too; it's not only them having a hard time understanding us."

"Tell me more about that—what do you mean?" Liz asked him, trying to better understand his experience. As a native English speaker, Liz was interested in this new perspective.

"English is their first language and it seems like they don't realize that we all speak broken English. Sometimes it feels like they don't make the effort to try to work with us to—how do you Americans say?—'level the playing field.' They will speak really very fast and use a lot of expressions that we don't totally understand. It makes me really frustrated and angry sometimes." Pierre looked down at his hands as if a bit embarrassed that he had just expressed his frustrations to one of "them"—a native English speaker.

Liz sensed his hesitation. "I don't think you speak broken English. I am listening to you speaking very clearly and easily right now. Where did you get the impression that your English is broken?"

Pierre looked up at Liz and sensed her genuine interest. "Well, I guess it is because of my accent, and I get really nervous and I always feel so stressed. I am an executive expected to make presentations all of the time in English. I usually have to prepare a lot. I spend hours and hours preparing slides to make sure the English is right. I always practice with my wife, and it's a lot of work. Even after all that work it often feels that people don't understand what I am trying to say. I want people to see me as an innovator and a top contributor, but I'm not sure they do. On the team there are so many native speakers of English, and they seem to present with such ease. My boss—a native English speaker of course—has given me feedback that I need to improve, but I feel that his feedback is just holding me back. I feel very judged by my boss whenever I make presentations. When I present at trade shows, or when I'm invited to speak about our company, some people will come and tell me that I have such a great accent, but frankly I'd like for them to come and comment on what I have just said, instead of how I sounded saying it." Pierre laughed suddenly. "Ahh, I am so sorry to bore you with such details."

Liz laughed along with Pierre. "Well, your boss should go to Brazil and try his English there. I used to give feedback to my non-native speakers of English just like your boss gives you. But now, I actually feel more like you," Liz said with a huge smile on her face. She laughed again. "I too am an executive, and we are in the same boat. Just a few weeks ago I gave a presentation. Even though the official language of the company is English, I'm not sure the audience understood me. I was just seeing a sea of empty faces. I felt a little shattered! I am surrounded by Portuguese speakers who are working in English with me, but I am clearly at a major disadvantage."

Pierre looked at her thoughtfully. "Thank you for sharing that, because I do not hear that too often. I often feel that we—the non-native speakers of English—do all the hard work. We take accent reduction courses and conversation classes, all after long days at work." He laughed again. "What I would dream of is for native English speakers to develop some skills to be more comfortable with different cultures and accents. I'm okay to work hard, but they could meet us halfway. I want you to be at ease in Brazil, but I must confess how wonderful it is to hear a native speaker struggling in English!"

Pierre and Liz both burst out laughing. Pierre continued, "I see this problem in many companies in Asia. They spend hours and hours on accent reduction and work on their pitch—all of those painful things. I have a friend in Japan who's a genius—he really is—but a lot of Americans are having a hard time understanding him. He's totally brilliant and should be a part of the executive team. I think he has equal skills or even better skills than some of the current leaders, but he's not promoted because of his accent."

Pierre and Liz had been so wrapped up in their conversation they didn't realize how crowded the airport lounge had become. Almost all the tables were filled with travelers frustrated with their long layovers. A dark-haired man had been sitting at the table next to Liz sipping on his scotch and trying to hide his overt interest in their conversation.

"I am so sorry, but I overheard what you said," the man said to Pierre and Liz.

Pierre and Liz were both now becoming aware that the lounge was cramped and the crowd was growing. They looked over at the man.

"I apologize, but it is very interesting to me," continued the man. "What you say is so true for me as well. I'm so sorry for interrupting. I just find it very interesting that you are talking about this. I have many friends in companies who are very frustrated because they don't feel they can express themselves well in English."

Liz and Pierre shared a glance. "Don't apologize!" said Liz. "Do *you* have the same frustrations at work? Your English sounds fine!"

The man's eyes widened and he brought his index finger near the tip of his nose and tapped into the air three times. "Me?" he asked Liz.

Liz furrowed her eyebrows slightly. "Yes, yes, you. Do you have a hard time at work?"

"Well, like many Japanese it is really very difficult for us. We often sit in meetings and can't follow the meaning very well. Then there is what people call 'brainstorming,' but it just seems like people are guessing in public and people speak all at the same time—or even try to speak over each other. It is not very organized." He hesitated. "I . . . I . . . I find it very difficult. I have gotten some cultural training where people told me this would happen, but I find it very frustrating, and I don't understand how this way is useful."

Liz sat back in her seat and chuckled. "It's funny you say that, because when I worked in the U.S. brainstorming was second nature to me. But the first time I ran a meeting in Brazil, I opened up the chance for brainstorming and I was the only one speaking! It made me feel very uncomfortable."

In disbelief, the Japanese man asked, "In Brazil?"

"Oh yeah! I thought brainstorming was second nature for people, but now I'm learning exactly what you're learning. What's your name, by the way?" asked Liz.

"I am Toshi." He paused. "Yes, it is very difficult for me. And I worry sometimes how I will then get my ideas so quickly out in English. I really admire my American colleagues for just being able to speak to strangers, but for us Japanese it is very difficult."

Pierre, sitting at the end of the bar, turned toward Toshi and asked, "Are you in a position where you have to speak up in meetings?"

"Yes, yes. I get feedbacks from my boss that I must speak more and contribute to team meetings, and all of that has to do with speaking. Sometimes I struggle to find when to start saying something because everyone talks already. I even don't know when to enter. Sometimes it takes me some time to express my ideas, and then I do not find the opportunity to respectfully inject my point of view. I am even more embarrassed since I am a vice president, and they expect to hear words from me."

Liz chuckled and, shifting her gaze to Pierre, said, "American people are excellent at interrupting people." Pierre added, "Well—the French do it, too!"

Liz and Pierre burst into laughter, and Toshi smiled slightly and said, "Yes, but that is impolite in my culture."

Liz's laughter turned into a smile as she answered, "There is a way to do it gracefully, I guess. But if you don't do it, you won't get your ideas across."

Toshi was still a bit uneasy with the direction of this conversation but felt comfortable expressing his true feelings after having overheard most of Liz and Pierre's previous conversation. "I feel that there are so many other ways for expressing your ideas—it doesn't always have to be in meetings in public, in front of everybody."

Pierre could relate to Toshi's struggle with this. "Many corporations are really looking to become more global, and I think that everyone should recognize the extra effort it takes for non-native English speakers to work and lead in English. Frankly, I am not seeing recognition, sympathy, or encouragement from any human resources people or direct leadership. It's not taken into consideration. It's not on their minds at all. Yes, English is the language of business, but if we really, truly want corporations to be global, we need to address this question and acknowledge that there is work to do on both sides and get more support. I'm not talking about learning specific things in English—most of us speak English well enough. I don't know if Einstein spoke perfect English, but he was making remarkable presentations even with a heavy German accent."

Pierre paused to take a quick sip of his sparkling mineral water that had finally arrived. "A good friend of mine—he is Greek—is one of the top experts in his field and is teaching in many universities around the world. One of his colleagues introduced him to a university in the U.S. and encouraged him to send over his resume to them. He sent an e-mail, and the person at the university basically said that based on his English and the grammar of his e-mail he would never be invited to teach at the university. I was finding it funny because it's as if someone had said to Einstein, 'Your accent is too hard to understand to teach in our university,'" Pierre said in a mocking voice.

Liz was surprised. "He lost the job because of it?"

"He didn't get the job, no. All because of his casual e-mail where his grammar wasn't perfect."

Toshi's eyes widened in surprise, but he remembered a time in his own company when grammar and the use of U.S. slang had caused a problem with a Japanese colleague of his.

"I also have one experience of a colleague who had a big problem because of a grammar issue—well, really it was the use of American slang. We have many American executives, and one of them came to Japan to make a presentation. He had a presentation slide that said in big letters G-O-T-C-H-A."

Toshi finished spelling the word and Liz quickly interrupted and giggled, "Oh! Gotcha!"

"Yes, gotcha," Toshi repeated. "My Japanese colleague, like many of the Japanese in my office, carries around an electronic dictionary, so he looked up what the meaning of 'gotcha' is and it did not come up in the dictionary. He was very upset that this American executive was making a presentation and using words that were not even in the dictionary. He actually got up from the meeting and left. The meeting was all about becoming a more global workplace and inspiring everyone to work hard to respect diversity in the organization, but using the word 'gotcha' was disrespectful to us, because we as Japanese had a very difficult time understanding or even finding the meaning in a dictionary."

Pierre and Liz both shook their heads disapprovingly. Liz asked, "What happened to your colleague who left the meeting?"

"Nothing. The American executive didn't think it was a sign of misunderstanding. Apparently many people in America leave meetings to take phone calls or do other work, so for him it was not a big problem."

Pierre and Liz both shrugged their shoulders, acknowledging that in the United States that happens frequently: people leave meetings, and nobody thinks twice about it.

"I have a good friend of mine whose name is Frederic," Pierre began. "He was working for a joint venture between a French company and an American company in the aeronautics industry. The leader was very visionary; he wanted to have 50 percent American employees and 50 percent French employees, and he sent the French people to America and vice versa. When he was giving presentations in America he would make sure that the French people were heard. I think he is like . . . what is the expression—hmm, a poster child for what leadership should be—it really is the leader's responsibility to be, well . . . inclusive."

Pierre, Liz, and Toshi all nodded their heads in agreement. A short silence in the conversation led them all to become aware of their surroundings. The lounge had become packed with travelers, many of whom were now sitting on the floor as all the seats at the bar and the tables were filled. A woman standing at the bar with her hand in the air caught Pierre's eye. He watched as she tried many times to get the attention of the bartender, but with no luck she slowly put her hand to her side and stood looking for a seat.

"Wait a minute—I'll be right back," said Pierre.

Pierre slid off the barstool he was currently occupying, making sure to leave his slightly crinkled jacket there so as not to lose his place. He approached the woman to offer some help.

"Excuse me, madame. Do you need help to get the attention of the bartender?"

The woman looked up at Pierre. "Oh, I am just trying to order some food."

Pierre turned to the bar and in his loud, deep voice called over the bartender, "Bartender! Bartender! Can you come over when you are done? This woman has been standing here for a long while."

The bartender, still not fully understanding Pierre, made his way over to the end of the bar where the woman was standing.

"What can I help you with?" the bartender asked Pierre. Pierre looked over at the woman and the bartender's gaze shifted over to her as well.

"May I please have a mixed green salad with grilled chicken and salad dressing on the side?" the woman asked.

The bartender scribbled something in his notepad and walked away. The woman turned to Pierre and said, "Thank you! I could well be standing there for another 20 minutes!"

Pierre smirked. "You might still be standing there for a while. I ordered my food a long time ago and I still haven't gotten it, but you're welcome! I am Pierre. Where are you from?"

"I'm Wendy," responded the woman. "I am living and working in Dallas, but I originally came from China."

Pierre couldn't hide his excitement. "Wow! Would you like to join us while you wait for your food?"

She blushed with slight embarrassment, but said, "Yes! I'm on a four-hour delay here, so it would be great to share some company."

"It's funny because we were just talking about working in English. You may have your own stories," Pierre shared as they approached the table where Toshi and Liz sat.

"Liz and Toshi, this is Wendy. Wendy, this is Liz and Toshi. Toshi is from Japan but is working in the U.S. Liz is from the U.S. but works in Brazil. And Wendy here works in Texas but is from China!"

"Hi, Wendy! I'm so glad you are joining us! Like Pierre said, I am originally from the U.S., from New Jersey actually, and I moved to Brazil a few months ago. But my next assignment is in Shanghai. I was wondering if I need to take some courses to understand the Chinese culture—I'm used to working with international people, but would you advise me to take some courses in the U.S.?

"Yes," offered Wendy politely. "Any cultural program that you can take is wonderful. In my company, we have actually had a hard time finding programs for international professionals. If you can find one, I would definitely recommend taking it. I am going to be starting an accent modification program in two weeks."

"Really?" Pierre asked. "But your accent is so perfect—why would you waste your time in that program?"

"Well, a lot of people say that to me, but I . . . well, I was nominated for it within my company, and that's really the only program that my company offers. I really need to improve my communication skills," Wendy replied. "I did take a two-day course on living and working in the U.S. It was fun, but I am not sure how much of that information was useful."

Pierre fired back, "I find it very odd that you should take an accent modification class, because you are so fluent. It sounds crazy to me!" He now tried to bring everyone into the conversation. "Liz, I have been working in so many countries—in Japan, Thailand, Argentina—all over the world, and I'm not sure that I—well, I have taken courses to understand cultures, but they're really so superficial. What I understand is that there is an international code and there is a certain behavior that works pretty well in every culture. I am not an expert, Toshi, on Japanese culture, and in a two-day course I wouldn't become an expert! What are your thoughts, Toshi, about the culture course?"

Toshi thought for a moment, and then replied, "I think it is very helpful to learn about other people and how they think and behave, and maybe my company has given some interesting courses, but I always found that what people say about American culture and what is actually happening in a culture are two very different things. I would ask people who live in America about things that were said in the class, and they would disagree with what the trainer was telling us. It was a bit confusing for me, just like with the brainstorming I was talking about earlier—knowing that in America people brainstorm didn't make a difference for me when I was actually put in that situation. So it is not so helpful."

Wendy jumped in. "I was in a program once where they were speaking to Americans about doing business in China. My experience was not so good. I am from China. I grew up there, and all my family is there. The teacher was saying things about China that were so untrue and insulting. They were all based on generalization—China is a big country! I agree, classes like that not only do not give any skills, but they often do worse by giving the wrong first impression for people who haven't even been there before. It often also reinforces stereotypes and makes them stronger—it really can put more barriers in place. Now sometimes I feel that people look at me differently and think of me as 'Chinese' in a stereotypical way in my company."

Pierre shook his head in understanding, "Yeah, exactly. Although France is a smaller country, I pick up books on 'the French' and it's just a caricature. It's not very helpful. They should not be talking about big stereotypes and should instead be paying more attention to the relationship you have with people. All of these courses are trying to get outsiders to become like the others. If you try to fit in like that, then you will probably never succeed."

Toshi waited a few minutes until there was a natural pause in the conversation and added, "Yes, yes, yes; you could never become a Japanese." Everyone broke into spontaneous laughter. Toshi smiled, hoping he had not insulted anyone.

Liz, who had kept fairly quiet and listened to the struggles of her newfound friends, asked a question that seemed obvious to the rest of them: "Do you all have to give presentations in front of people in English?"

Pierre was the first to respond. "Yes, of course! I spend probably a third of my time making presentations in English."

Wendy followed. "I wish I had a better ability to do it, but I just got promoted and I will be speaking in front of native English speakers on a regular basis. My feedback from my boss is that I speak so quietly that nobody hears me. I'd rather hide behind the podium. I hope my accent class can help me with this, though."

Pierre asked Wendy, "Are you more concerned with presenting in front of native English speakers or with non-native speakers, or is it the same for both?"

"I think it is the same for both. Where I am in the company, the value is for the leaders to be able to speak well in public, and I think that this is where my failure will come," Wendy answered. "I think it is very stressful, and it seems so much easier for European colleagues. They learned English much earlier, and somehow it seems to be easier for them. I find it difficult. I also have such a small vocabulary . . . ."

Pierre interrupted Wendy. "Is it easier for you to present in your native language, Toshi and Wendy? Is it easier for you than having to present in an international context?"

"Well, I have never worked in my native language," Wendy responded. "So, I think it is easier for me in English. I have confidence in Mandarin, but I've been in Dallas for 15 years, so all of my presentation experience is in English."

"I give presentations in Japanese to colleagues in Japan often," said Toshi. "It is easier. I still prepare a lot, but it is much easier to present my thoughts and my research in Japanese. In fact, I'm on my way to give a presentation in Japan, and I'm looking forward to doing it in Japanese."

Wendy continued to discuss her struggles with presenting in both English and Mandarin with Toshi. Liz leaned over to Pierre and whispered, "Where is your hamburger?"

Pierre looked around. "I was just wondering the same thing! Probably in the same place as your snack menu."

Both chuckled.

Our lounge companions fell into a comfortable silence as they waited for their food and reflected on each other's stories. The lounge became more crowded and louder. Unknown to our group, a woman sat behind them, listening to their conversation and smiling mysteriously.

To be continued . . .

1

It Takes Two
to Tango

Tango requires effort and patience and the willingness to learn. But, the rewards are awesome. A connection with another human being that some describe as . . . a dance of communication and connection.

—Florintino Guizar[1]

Pierre, Liz, Toshi, and Wendy reflect the many faces of international professionals* working in English. As we have seen, they encounter

---

*The phrase *international professionals* was first used by Vince in the late 1990s after working with hundreds of native and non-native speakers of English who were struggling to communicate effectively in their respective organizations. He felt the term "ESL" (English as a Second Language) employees only referred to non-native speakers who needed baseline help in English. The term captured neither the advanced non-native nor the native speakers working in multilingual environments. Hence, he coined the phrase "international professionals" and has used it to help organizations identify this specific group of individuals and address their unique set of challenges.

hurdles on the path to success because of the interplay of language and culture in global business. They want to inspire, encourage, and motivate others to reach their full abilities. They are all dedicated leaders, fast-trackers, high potentials, and star performers who share a common bond: English is driving them crazy!

Throughout their discussions we uncover some of the under-lying emotions and ongoing challenges that reinforce their experi-ences. In the workplace, they are out of step and struggle to be authentic, effective, and included. Each is clearly on a leadership track, but that path is clouded as their talents and abilities are hidden while their confidence is stifled because of linguistic and cultural boundaries.

Yet, together they find a bond and a collective wisdom. Our international friends reflect on their situations not with despair, but with humor, social grace, and goodwill. They find hope in one another's stories. They recognize themselves as seasoned leaders managing complex businesses in an interdependent world. They rally around their common frustrations and find an outlet where they can express their stories to a sympathetic audience. Even though working in English causes anxiety and insecurity, they are motivated leaders and up for the challenge. They simply need better solutions, and their organizations need a clearer vision of how to handle the phenomenon of the widespread use of English.

How widespread? According to Mark Robson of the British Council, "English is spoken at a useful level by some 1.75 billion people worldwide—that's one in every four. By 2020, we forecast that 2 billion people will be using it."[2] Clearly, English is becoming the language of choice for global conversations.

In addition to the staggering number of people using English worldwide, a *Newsweek* article titled "Not the Queen's English" indicated that, as early as 2005, non-native speakers of English outnumber native English speakers 3 to 1.[3] A recent *Wall Street Journal* article stated that "almost one in 10 adults of working age in the U.S. has limited proficiency in English, more than 2.5 times as many as in 1980."[4] These staggering numbers indicate that the spread of English has been changing methods of communication and will impact global organizations in their talent-retention strategies, workforce-development initiatives, and diversity and inclusiveness processes. If the axiom is true that people drive the success of an organization, then such success depends on the interactions of both native and non-native speakers of English.

Our focus in *Leading in English* is on the seasoned international professionals who work in English every day—native and non-native speakers of English alike. Most of the solutions available in the marketplace focus on the beginning or intermediate non-native communicators—those who still need to build their foundation in English. Very little attention is paid to the advanced native and non-native speakers working across language and cultures.

Our audience for this book includes the following:

- The non-native-speaking* global leaders who are working in English in:
  - Their home countries
  - Global, multilingual environments
  - English-speaking countries, leading a native-speaking workforce
  - English-speaking countries, reporting to a native-speaking boss
- Native-speaking* global leaders who are working in:
  - Countries where English is the business language but not the local language (like Liz)
  - Global, multilingual environments

---

*When we use the terms *native-speaking* and *non-native speaking*, we are referring to English unless specifically noted.

- Home countries—United States, United Kingdom, Australia—leading a multilingual workforce
- Home countries, reporting to a non-native speaker

So why does English cause so many problems even for these professionals who are already strong or even native in English? Our airport-lounge characters certainly fit the profile, and we will examine their stories. But we begin with a suggested mind-set shift. A very useful idiom that we have in English is that "it takes two to tango," which will serve as our new mantra in this book. The tango is an energetic dance that requires both partners to be highly attuned to each other in an interplay of responsive movements—"a dance of communication and connection,"[5] as Florintino Guizar, an expert in Argentine tango, describes.

Another well-known English idiom is "When in Rome, do as the Romans do." This idiom suggests that people should behave like the native people of any given environment. Originally, it referred to the dominance that the Romans once had in the world and the expectation that outsiders should conform to their norms. Not too dissimilar is our current status quo, which—perhaps not overtly stated—is that people who speak English should adapt to Anglo-Saxon norms, not only linguistically but also behaviorally. Yet it may take years before a non-native speaker can fully understand what those norms entail. At the heart of this discourse is the relationship that exists between people who do not speak the same native language and whose accents communicate that they are not from here (wherever here may be).

Leading in English strives to change the international business code from "when in Rome, do as the Romans do" to the more inclusive thought behind the concept "it takes two to tango."

When a relationship is founded on trust and a level playing field, communication improves, regardless of the hierarchical status. But what does it mean to "level the playing field"? Many global organizations that are embracing diversity and inclusion seek solutions to help the non-native speakers. These are very useful and necessary initiatives.

However, very few solutions are provided to help native and non-native speakers better understand each other. It takes two to tango. We support a new set of standards for using English that reinforces both groups. We further want to ensure that the purpose of communication is to understand an intended message rather than to make hasty judgments about how the messages are sent. Language limitations are not personality or intellectual defects. They are also not a reflection of personal incapability or cultural disrespect. Our aim is to reduce misunderstanding, accept a certain amount of ambiguity, and create tools and strategies to better communicate. Period.

Leading in English represents many stories from various international professionals who both struggle and succeed in English. As a point of reference for the reader, "we" and "our" collectively represent the three authors of the book. Vince Varallo, a native English speaker, consults with Fortune 500 companies and has trained and coached thousands of international professionals. Joerg Schmitz, a native German speaker, is a cultural anthropologist with extensive experience helping leaders and organizations navigate the challenges and opportunities of globalization. Stephan Mardyks, a native French speaker, is a world-renowned expert in the field of global learning and development.

During our journey, we have asked numerous international professionals to reflect on their own relationship with the English language. We'll be sharing many of their stories in the pages to come. Most of the stories come from the perspective of non-native English speakers, but we have also collected interesting examples from native speakers who struggle expressing themselves, especially in public.

Here is an example that we find quite illuminating. Stephan learned about it from a friend, who is a native French speaker:

Despite speaking perfect French (having been born and raised in Paris), I was not seen as "true French" by most of the people I went to school with and later by my colleagues at work. As the first generation born in France, from a Dutch family, I was just different.

Actually, some people would say—"You're so-o-o not French!"

I quickly understood that I needed to work for international corporations where success is based on personal achievements, not where you come from.

Traveling, meeting and working with different cultures across the world, was invigorating to me, and I was not seen as only "French" but more as a cosmopolitan person. Working in English as non-English speakers was "part of the job" and a nonissue for most of us.

Promoted in my early thirties as VP, I had been asked to lead the global strategy and operations of a new venture based in Atlanta. Part of my job was to lead a global network and an American staff.

My English was okay in a professional context, but not so great for the folks taking my order at the fried chicken and grits restaurant next door. Granted, being dressed in an Italian suit and tie with some French cologne was probably not the best camouflage.

I clearly understood that I had been given this leadership position not only due to my potential but also to help people be more globally minded. I was indeed the perfect alien for the job to be done.

When everyone was playing "Monday morning quarterback," it took me a little bit of time to understand that they were not talking about American football. How confusing.

I always had this belief that the American dream was also about "melting together." But I totally missed the fact that it does not apply if you have a foreign accent. You have access to the pot but you can't melt.

Nothing was about my skills and know-how anymore—everything, all day long, was about my thick French accent and perceived French persona.

Yes, I know what you're thinking: not the worst accent to have; but try to understand—all day long I heard "you're so-o-o French!"

So, here I am, leaving the French culture for not being French enough, just to become the ultimate aristocratic Frenchman in Atlanta.

I spent so much time and effort trying to fit in and reduce my accent. I wanted so badly to be seen and heard for what I had to say—not the way I was saying it. It was exhausting. Not only did I have my day job like the others, but I also had to deal with my accent and the endless feedback about it.

The biggest compliment at that time was being asked if I was Canadian—at least that was getting closer!

One day—after a critical business presentation in front of the most important executives of our multinational—I realized that I would never be seen for who I am, but would always be seen as an outsider.

In my mind, I was NIH—Not Invented Here.

I was so discouraged that day that I came back home, opened the front door, and immediately went and collapsed on my bed.

I was thinking—What do I do? Do I go back to France? But I was an outsider there, too.

Good thing that I'm not a drinker. By the way, I'm a Frenchman who does not drink wine but can explain the taste difference between Pepsi and Coke . . . but that's another story.

And then in the middle of the night I had this epiphany—my style and accent are going to become my brand, just like Henry Kissinger.

I was going to be myself and not try any longer to belong at any cost. My accent was part of who I was and I would stop focusing on the issues related to it. From now on I would just be myself. Take it or leave it!

The morning after, I regained my confidence and freedom. I did belong—not because I was part of any old boys' club, but because I could contribute and do good.

I became (as I was told) a much better leader in the U.S., and for some reason my accent became just a detail—not a "definer." In hindsight, I think that I was part of the problem.

His transformation from discouraged outsider to confident leader came when he stopped trying to fit in and learned to value his own unique identity and the distinctive contribution he could make. His focus shifted from reducing his accent to leading his team, and once he made that shift he unlocked a new reservoir of energy. We've seen a similar result in the lives of many international professionals as they learn a new way to navigate the world of English.

We use the term *English* both in a literal sense—referring to the actual language—and in the wider metaphorical sense, referring to the dominant medium of communication that defines relationships and meaning, which is symbolically tied to the history and culture of English speakers. All of us can use the English language explosion to enhance our careers, motivate others, and embrace the spirit of inclusion. However, we must not fall prey to thinking that English in business means we should conduct ourselves as U.S. Americans, Canadians, or Brits.

The easy assumption is that to use English we should adopt the behavioral norms and behaviors of the people who use it the most. When in Rome, do as the Romans do. Whether the thought process is conscious or unconscious, the prevailing status quo is that "if you communicate in English, you should conduct business like we do." The reality is that the business world is accepting English as its lingua franca, but not necessarily adopting a new way of life; the language shift does not come paired with an automatic cultural shift. Miscommunication often comes not just from language but also from the combination of using English across many cultures and business situations.

Every single day, people on global teams from multiple countries and from various language backgrounds are using English to connect with one another, manage complex ideas, and move their companies toward profitability. Like a garden hose without a nozzle, the ideas stream from one person to the next, from one group to the other. They flow from interactions including face-to-face meetings, web-based conferences, e-mail messaging, social media, teleconferences, texting, and so forth. While the levels of ambiguity might be high, people rally around the essential themes, derive their action plans, and move their agendas ahead.

Amidst this flood of English, even native speakers can unexpectedly be at a disadvantage. A chemist from northern New Jersey, Bob, recently explained to a group of other native-speaking colleagues that he—as the only native English speaker on his team of eight—struggles the most in understanding the team's direction. The group wanted to know how that could possibly be. Well, the garden hose is streaming ideas without a filter. Grammar mistakes are made, accents are diverse, and ambiguity runs high—all characteristics that native speakers fight against, but all common traits among the non-native speakers. They use English as a delivery platform and not as a way of life. The other native speakers wanted to know: "Don't you have a high degree of miscommunication? Aren't deadlines missed?" Bob's answer was most interesting: "Of course we do. But no more than when I work with a team of all native speakers."

So why is communication in English easier for non-native speakers working with one another? Logic might tell us that native speakers would be able to convey their thoughts more clearly to non-native speakers. In our research with participants from around the world, we have found the opposite to be true. Because native speakers communicate with a shared set of symbols and codes—most of which are intuitive—non-native speakers can be at a loss when communicating with them.

You can see the intuitive understanding that native speakers have with one another in the following dialogue between two native speakers in a New York office:

Bill: Hey, I just heard that the marketing department has been told they can work from home on Fridays. We should do that, don't you think? I can talk to Linda [the boss].

Sharon: Hmm. [Sharon tilts her head and raises her eyebrows.] You'd better be careful. You know how traditional Linda can be. Listen, I'm off running to a meeting. We can talk more about that later if you want.

Bill reads Sharon's body language, recognizes her hesitation, and decides to hold off on his suggestion. Message received by Bill: he had better not ask Linda about possibly working from home on Fridays.

Now, take the same interaction with Hector, who has recently arrived from Mexico. In his cross-cultural training program, he has been told to be proactive and share his ideas. He is an outgoing fellow and wants to fit in right away. His slight grammatical mistakes are reflected here.

Hector: Hello, Sharon. The marketing department have been approved to work from their home on Friday. What a good idea. I should talk to Linda [the boss] to see if it is a good idea for us.

Sharon: Hmm. [Sharon tilts her head and raises her eyebrows.] You'd better be careful. You know how traditional Linda can be. Listen, I'm off running to a meeting. We can talk more about that later if you want.

Hector thinks, "Well, I did consider this carefully as Sharon suggested, so I should approach Linda in a very structured way." He decides to speak with her about the idea. Hector did not correctly read Sharon's body language. He also did not pick up on the cue that Linda is very traditional and might not be receptive to having the group work from home on Fridays. Message received by Hector: he should carefully construct his message when speaking with Linda.

Now let's examine the same interaction with Hector and Chen, who is from China and has been in the United States for three years.

Hector: Hello, Chen. The marketing department have been approved to work from their home on Friday. What a good idea. I should talk to Linda [the boss] to see if it is a good idea for us.

Chen: Hmm. [Chen frowns.] I'm not sure such good idea. Maybe you should not hold meeting.

Hector understands all the negative cues, appreciates Chen's advice, and decides not to approach the boss. Message received by Hector: he had better not approach Linda about this idea.

The hose has no filter, and the thoughts—while not linguistically perfect—come out pure. Non-native speakers are at a disadvantage when working with native speakers who fully understand all the hidden codes and messages. As we have seen from Bob the chemist, native English speakers can also be at a disadvantage when working globally, whether on an intact team at home or on assignment in another country. Liz is discovering the challenge of using English where her filter—the nozzle on the hose—is different from the filters of those with whom she is communicating. Shortly, we will look at Liz and her dilemma.

Because of the missed cues, a lack of confidence on both sides prevails. The impact can be severe for non-native speakers, who are often overlooked for promotions, not chosen to face clients, and not encouraged to participate in important direction-setting meetings. There are many reasons why. Perhaps the lead manager does not believe an individual is ready for the complexity of the communication needed. In addition, the engagement team might not believe the client will accept a person with an accent as a credible voice. The individual contributor can also lack confidence and thus not speak up for fear of making a mistake or freezing up in a key situation.

We fully realize that most non-native speakers living in an English-speaking country want to adapt to the local norms, understand the cultural cues, and become strong communicators. Simply look at Wendy's situation. She not only needs to embrace English, but also needs to do it in a way that satisfies her colleagues in Dallas. We do not shy away from that reality. In fact, we support these professionals, like Wendy, by focusing on how they can develop stronger English in business, social, and everyday interactions. They want to advance their careers and contribute to the success of their organizations. In turn, the organizations that value diversity and inclusion are implementing solutions that help the non-native speakers.

Yet, it takes two to tango. These international professionals are only 50 percent of the equation. Does Wendy's leadership team in Dallas:

- Attempt to better understand her language and culture?
- Realize how hard it is for her to adjust to not only the linguistic, but also the cultural and business norms?
- Ask themselves what that might be like for them if they lived in China?
- Sponsor any orientation programs about how to best communicate with non-native speakers?

Perhaps an empathic approach might help them to understand the great success Wendy is already experiencing. We encourage native speakers to develop stronger relationships with non-native speakers by first recognizing that the filters—the nozzles on the hose—do not come naturally. Once both sides of the communication equation embrace each other's strengths and challenges, we foresee global enterprises:

- Recognizing and retaining their talent
- Uncovering hidden assets by helping people gain confidence in English
- Setting clear expectations
- Developing higher-performing teams
- Forging stronger synergies

We have hard work ahead of us. We are not promoting English as the preferred language but rather as the platform for international professionals to understand one another, to ensure that their delivered message will actually be their intended message. Yet we must be mindful of the fact that as a platform for global business, English creates inequities, barriers, and challenges that, if not navigated carefully, will undermine the collective experience, potential, and performance.

The struggle begins when we put the Anglo-Saxon nozzle on the hose and expect everyone to adapt and understand the filtered messages. By embracing new strategies, tactics, and solutions, together we can dance the tango—that high-energy dance—in rhythm. *Leading in English* helps to establish a mind-set shift and create new standards for using English.

What are some of those strategies? We have broken down the learning needs for international professionals—both native and non-native speakers—into a three-step progression for improving communication and effectiveness. *Leading in English* is organized along these three steps.

Speaking Clearly—It's about You

This first layer gets the most attention in organizations. Accent modification—while sometimes needed—is overly recommended and not always necessary. Many people have strong accents but are easily understood, whereas others have mild accents and sound muffled. In these cases, the focus should be on clarity of speech. While individuals can benefit from a personal learning plan to correct any articulation or pronunciation issues, their primary focus should be on developing confidence.

Speaking with Impact—It's about Them

The second layer represents a personal shift where the speaker no longer worries about her English, but rather focuses on her audience by answering the question: What does this listener or group of listeners need from me to best understand this interaction? Perhaps it is speaking more slowly on the telephone or speaking with more emphasis and vocal variety during a meeting or presentation. Impact learning involves increasing one's range of expression so that the audience pays attention to the message.

Developing a Compelling Narrative—It's about Moving Them

The final layer is the leadership piece that helps to motivate a group toward action. Leaders create connection by understanding the power of visualization through examples, scenarios, and targeted storytelling. Furthermore, they deliver concise, compelling messages that are sincere and activating.

Let's examine how these steps relate to our characters in the introductory chapter. By taking a deeper look at Pierre, Liz, Wendy, and Toshi, we provide an opportunity to investigate some challenging experiences that international professionals face while working in English.

First we have the bartender, who is a native speaker of English. Then come our international professionals, who are native speakers of French, English, Mandarin, and Japanese, respectively. They are quite fluent and advanced in English, a necessary skill for executives doing critical business around the world. All of them are accustomed to dealing with high levels of complexity, and seek better solutions for communicating in English. We further explore the various contextual situations that lead to their frustrations. Our task in *Leading in English* is to provide the tools needed to ensure successful communication across language and cultural boundaries.

Here are the characters and the archetypes they represent:

The Bartender (native speaker), "The Wall": His real name is Steven. The bartender stands in the way of Pierre and his lunch order. Nothing will be accomplished since the bartender hears "accent" only, quickly shuts down active listening, and fails to understand the intended message. The bartender represents old-school thinking: he hears an accent and assumes, perhaps unconsciously, that the person has less intelligence, education, and capability. Even after Pierre's multiple attempts, the bartender remains confused until a third party—in this case Liz—clarifies the order. The bartender is a metaphor for someone who stands in the way of successful communication for international professionals.

Pierre, "The Misunderstood": Pierre is not thrilled when the simple act of ordering a cheeseburger doesn't go as planned. While the interaction in the lounge frustrates Pierre, we later find out that in business situations as well he feels inadequate, loses confidence, and fosters some resentment. His accent in English—and the way people listen to his accent—is causing him frustration.

Liz, "The Surprised Native Speaker": Liz is speaking in her mother tongue but having a hard time connecting with the Brazilians she works with. While she was expecting to struggle with Portuguese, she did not anticipate having trouble in English. Liz is like the many native speakers working globally in non-English-speaking countries.

Wendy, "The Confused": Her real name in Mandarin is Wenling. Wendy wants to get better in English. She lives and works in Dallas and has been identified for accent modification classes. However, she is always being told that her accent is easy to understand. Neither the organization nor Wendy understands how she could improve her overall communication skills. Wendy already performs well in certain areas of English, but those talents go unrecognized. She is at a loss for what to do next.

Toshi, "The Unheard": His full name is Toshihiro. Toshi sits quietly in brainstorming sessions as his mind races to figure out a way to go about sharing his thoughts. He was not asked to prepare anything for the discussion. He sits patiently and watches as all the native speakers interrupt one another with great ease. Toshi quickly but quietly becomes frustrated. He does not want to be rude. On the other hand, if he does not participate, he may be perceived as being ill prepared for the meeting. It's a double-edged sword.

Let's begin by examining the various interactions among our characters.

Pierre just couldn't seem to make the bartender understand his order. Many observers may note that Pierre was in the United States, so he had the ultimate responsibility to be understood in English. When in Rome, do as the Romans do. Well, we believe that it takes two to tango. Why couldn't the bartender seek to clarify and help Pierre? Easy solutions were available to assist in the food order to ensure that the intended message would become the received message. That interaction should have been easy. In this context, the bartender failed to make any extra effort. On the other hand, Pierre was stubborn; he could also have made that interaction easier. The communication went awry. In other situations, we recognize there are times when both sides are motivated to understand each other but can't cut through the barriers. The reader should note that speaking clearly, the first level of our learning system, includes both the speaker being more clear and the listener making a better effort to understand.

In Chapter 2, we will go into greater depth about the dilemma of accents.

Let's examine Liz and her challenges. She is the wild card in the group as the only native speaker, but, interestingly, her challenges are not that dissimilar to those of the other characters.

"What am I to do?" she thinks. "When the company declared English as the official language, I thought that it was a lucky break. However, I find myself being misunderstood all the time. My team and I are behind on work, and we can't seem to catch up. I am not getting through to them. I took the company course on doing business in Brazil. I am following those baseline principles, but, honestly, they do not really help. I'll never give up, but this is more difficult than I thought it would be."

A common assumption about native speakers is that they are confident in their English language capabilities, but we know many who struggle to communicate effectively. Frustration sets in when they are met with quizzical looks and empty stares. They use numerous idioms and do not realize that such phrasing might not be understood. Some speak far too quickly. Liz tries to speak slowly, but the last thing she wants to do is become condescending and act like a teacher working with grade-school children. She also feels lost when her team speaks in Portuguese right in front of her. "Are they speaking about me? Mocking me? Is there something they don't want me to know?" She understands cognitively that these questions reflect far more insecurity than reality; however, emotionally she feels like an outsider, which makes her anxious.

Interestingly, her lounge colleagues are surprised that she is having difficulty communicating in Brazil. They can't fathom that Liz feels disadvantaged. Pierre in particular finds this intriguing and, with good humor, he is almost happy to hear it. He and Liz got a good laugh out of that as they realized their issues were not as dissimilar as they may have thought. Trying to be a good leader, Liz wants to strip away any ambiguity and connect with her Brazilian direct reports. She has a positive attitude but knows that she has not formed a strong team because of the inequity in English. Both sides need a strategy to help them bring synergy to their work and their relationships.

Liz supports non-native speakers when needed. After all, she readily stepped in and helped Pierre order his food. Pierre could have been insulted by Liz's interference, but he appreciated her efforts. Why can't Liz reverse the process and help her Brazilian colleagues understand her English? Well, it takes two to tango. We are unsure of the English level of the Brazilians she is working with; however, we do know that neither side is making the necessary adjustments. The intended message is lost, and communication is faltering. Having worked with leading executives around the world, we are told by many that a lack of collaboration and poor communication are the heart of failed projects. The "us" versus "them" mentality must change before problems can be solved.

Liz represents "them" and is clearly an outsider in Brazil. No one has ever explained to her the best approach for working with non-native speakers. But she represents—to the locals—the dominant role of U.S. culture; thus, the use of English also makes them feel like outsiders. The insider/outsider experience is at the heart of developing inclusive mind-sets and behaviors in the global workforce. The dynamics change based on the context and are often quite complex. Liz does not feel like an insider when working in Brazil—and certainly from a social perspective she is an outsider. She needs help to navigate the never-ending tasks of relocating to another country. She must develop strong outsider skills by getting closer to the native groups and understanding the rhythms of the local environment. However, she must also understand the challenges her Brazilian team faces when she uses English. Just as Liz is an outsider to the culture, they are outsiders to the language.

Maja Egnel, vice president of talent development and diversity at Skanska, states:

An outsider will often experience a lack of control, and feel weak, confused, vulnerable, and frustrated. Outsiders are expected to adhere to the rules set by the insiders, and must work harder than insiders for the same opportunities. They will spend a lot of energy trying to be accepted by the insider group, and they are often less engaged, motivated, and satisfied.

The insider experience, on the other hand, is very different, since most insiders might not even realize their insider status. The insider group has the formal or informal power to create the rules, and will be the ones reinforcing compliant behavior . . . . In fact, not feeling valued and included has a deteriorating effect on performance as well as commitment and company loyalty.[6]

Liz is a bright executive and a strong leader who has both people and project management skills. She will manage both her insider and outsider roles. International professionals are chosen because of their adaptability and are usually the cream of the crop, resilient souls who know how to adjust and prepare for success. We want to support Liz and the millions of other international professionals working in English across borders and boundaries by advocating communication strategies to use English that fosters understanding and enhances inspiration. Liz needs to be clear in her speech, deliver impact in her messages, and develop a strong narrative.

Let's turn next to Wendy, known as Wenling in Mandarin. Like many Chinese women living and working in the United States, she decided to take a coaching program to help with her communication skills. While she thought that the company's accent program might help a little, she decided to go with a more customized approach with a personal coach. After performing an evaluation of her overall skills, the coach determined that her accent and clarity of speech were effective. However, this only caused Wendy to become even more frustrated. She said, "While it is nice to know that I don't have a strong accent, I am still being judged by native speakers and my promotion will be denied unless I improve my English." She did not want to hear that language is a 50/50 proposition and that native speakers also must adjust. Wendy is realistic, knows her environment, and must improve.

But what adjustments does she need to make? Why is she so down and out about her English? Why does she lack confidence in all forms of her communication? Yes, she does tend to drop the "s" sound at the ends of words and does make some minor grammatical mistakes. However, she is clearly understood and has a strong enough vocabulary to describe virtually any situation around her. Nevertheless, she has little impact on her audience. While the easy recommendation is to follow the second stage of the learning plan—speaking with impact— most organizations and most of the professionals themselves are not aware of this level of learning.

Wendy's dilemma is a central theme in this book. She is not only expected to speak English fluently, but also expected to act like the other leaders around her. She wants to adapt and learn the necessary skills. However, Wendy is lacking pop and pizzazz in her messaging. Passion in English is displayed through vocal variety—the rising and falling of intonation, alternating speeds, and framing ideas. Wendy has been told to slow down her entire career and has thus turned into a monotone speaker. Her career advancement depends on this impact by gaining credibility with clients, influencing coworkers, and inspiring direct reports. The organization expects her to be a strong leader with solid skills, and she expects the same for herself. Wendy does not shy away from her perceived challenges. She embraces the additional opportunities to learn, just like so many international professionals.

These non-native speakers find themselves at the crossroads of business, language, and culture, but their challenges are often not understood or appreciated by the native speakers they work with. Wouldn't Wendy's occupational life be so much easier if the native speakers of English accepted the fact that she is doing so well in English? They could value her clear speaking and strong base of grammar. They could better understand that strong intonation is not a reflection of passion where Wendy comes from. Wendy's learning would be easier if her counterparts better understood what it feels like to communicate complex ideas daily in another language. That level of empathy is sorely lacking in most organizations.

A key insight here is that organizations in native-speaking countries unintentionally isolate international professionals by not recognizing and valuing their strengths. Performance reviews tear down their confidence and make them feel inadequate. Worst of all, neither Wendy nor the organization knows exactly how to help plan for her improvement. The immediate response is that non-native speakers need to reduce their accents. That knee-jerk reaction is causing trouble. It takes two to tango. It also takes two to build better performance improvement plans.

Unlike Wendy, who has lived in the United States for 15 years, Toshi has arrived recently and is far more comfortable in his native Japanese. He tries to understand the norms of American culture by "standing up and being counted," as he has been told. But he does not know what that means, nor does he know how or when to do that.

Toshi is having a hard time communicating in English. He also feels that the cultural classes he received did not help. In fact, all our professionals in the lounge agreed that the corporate solutions did not prepare them well for their global work. Toshi gets confused because the course content told him that Americans behave in a particular way, but then he has others tell him something different. To make matters more confusing, he finds the actual behaviors of Americans to be very different from both what he has been taught and what he has been told.

Interestingly, Toshi learned about brainstorming in culture classes, but he still does not understand the purpose and finds that the process has little value. Toshi's reaction to brainstorming is quite interesting. While business professionals in the United States view brainstorming as structured discussions, many non-native employees view it simply as chaos without a chance to interact. A French colleague marveled at one particular meeting when the U.S. facilitator said, "There are no dumb ideas." She leaned over and quietly said, "There are plenty of dumb ideas, and she just wrote one down."

Saying something without careful consideration is hard to imagine for Toshi. The thought of interrupting someone is even worse. One of his frustrations represents a huge challenge for non-native English speakers when working in English. "How exactly do I get a word in?" The Americans and the British seem to do it with ease. One of our U.S. colleagues laughed when he heard us discuss how challenging it is for second-language speakers to squeeze their way into a conversation. He said, "I never even thought about it. Interrupting is a national pastime in the U.S."

In fact, Toshi finds it quite distasteful. He is not alone, as many of our Canadian friends also find consistently "butting in" to be an annoying habit. Yet everyone who comes to English-speaking countries is told that you should participate. The phrase "stand up and be counted" is taught in almost every cross-cultural program. The problem is that when people get to the United States they have no idea how to do it. We work with many clients who have been living in the United States for years and have found this to be a huge challenge.

As an example, last year we had the opportunity to coach a Chinese scientist working in a major pharmaceutical company. Let's call her Ling. Her communication challenges, as explained by the organization, were accent and clarity of speech. However, once we evaluated Ling's skills we found her accent to be mild and her sound production problems minimal. These perceptions arose because she very rarely spoke up at meetings, kept hushed tones over the phone, and lacked confidence in her current skill set.

The perceptions did not reflect the reality, as we often discover. Interestingly, Ling's grammar was impeccable even though she rated herself as below average. Our coaches encouraged her to speak up at meetings and taught her to use some polite language to interject herself into business conversations. Ling explained how rude it felt to interrupt; she imagined her father's frowning face as she committed such a faux pas. However, we showed her some gracious and polite expressions to interject herself into a business conversation. We further encouraged her to increase her volume. We also noticed that she had no trouble speaking up and, being a brilliant woman, she had strong ideas to contribute. She was clearly ready to share her voice and be heard inside the organization.

A few weeks after the start of her coaching sessions, we got a call from her manager. First, the manager praised Ling's quick learning style and how she was now such a great contributor to the weekly status meetings. "But," she added hesitantly, "could you please explain to her that she does not have to speak quite so much. Who knew Ling was so long-winded?" We all had a good laugh at that—including Ling, who quickly learned to find the balance between when to speak and when to listen.

Toshi also told an interesting story about how one presenter showed a slide that said "GOTCHA," without explaining what the term meant to his non-native audience. Toshi's colleague was so annoyed by this lack of consideration that he left the room. We certainly feel that Toshi's colleague overreacted, but imagine if that presenter took the time to explain "gotcha" and recognized that there were second-language speakers in the room. Everyone would have then been on the same page and the meeting content could have been clearly understood by all participants.

How much better would it be for his team leader to understand this about Toshi. Perhaps she could ask Toshi, prior to the meeting, to prepare some remarks. Then during the meeting, she might invite Toshi to speak. The available tools are easy to access, but the spirit of exchange needs to be revamped. As the world gets smaller, we need to challenge the dictum "when in Rome, do as the Romans do." Improved communication happens when everyone understands that it takes two to tango.

In fact, millions of people around the world are facing the same dilemma as Wendy and Toshi. The world, whether or not it is fully embracing it, is choosing English as the language of business. In this book, we do not explore why. We also do not examine hypothetical questions such as what language might supplant English in the coming years. It's not that we don't care, but that we are responding to the practical dilemmas that international professionals face right now. They use English every day and must build their careers on it. The market addresses their challenges with a limited range of language learning options, and expects non-native speakers to flock to these programs. Some of the programs are well targeted, but most fail to address the sophisticated needs of advanced communicators. The solutions very rarely address the convergence that is impacting the three critical areas of communication: language, culture, and business.

In addition, very few solutions exist for native speakers because their problems are not recognized. The prevailing thinking is that native speakers have an advantage and that everyone else can take language-training programs to catch up. That simplistic thinking does not prepare native speakers for global business. They need to adjust to non-native speakers by understanding how to:

- Decipher accents
- Expect limited vocabularies
- Anticipate odd syntax
- Control speed of communication
- Manage tone and range of expression

Throughout *Leading in English*, we address the challenges and possible solutions for both native and non-native speakers. Furthermore, we use actual stories from these professionals to illustrate our key points.

In Chapter 2, we cover the role that accents play in global business and the impact on individuals who are having a hard time being understood.

In Chapter 3, we explore innovative solutions for international professionals to deliver impactful messages.

In Chapter 4, we examine the importance for leaders to develop a compelling narrative.

Throughout the book, we detail how international professionals can put all this information together and form a comprehensive plan that will establish a new standard for using English worldwide.

Happy reading. We hope that you find new strategies to enhance your relationships and improve your experiences in English.

2 | Speaking Clearly— It's about You

It's a lack of clarity that creates chaos and frustration. Those emotions are poison to any living goal.

—Steve Maraboli[1]

On one hand, speaking clearly seems like such an obvious goal for any communicator. When you are not clear, you should work on developing your personal communication abilities—that's why we chose the tagline "It's about you" to frame this discussion. However, that does not mean that your skills are the single source of the lack of clarity, or even that you should shoulder all the responsibility. A deeper look at our audiences reveals that "it takes two to tango."

When we speak with clarity, our intended message is the received message. Clarity is what our audiences crave when we represent ourselves in communication. In other words, clarity is in the mind of the beholder. One German professional who studied in the United States put it this way:

> How painstakingly I struggled with English, ever since I started to learn it at age 11. I was in a constant battle with my English teachers. In hindsight, I recognized that they didn't know how to deal with my learning style, and I was struggling to fit English into my cognitive structure. That failed miserably. I exhausted my English teachers with grammatical questions, and grew frustrated by their inability to "explain" the inconsistencies and irregularities of English (which, I believed, was the only way to make the language intelligible to me). I was resistant to simply accepting irregularity as a feature of English. But I struggled most of all with the sentence structure. I loved that in German I could mirror the structure of my thought in the structure of my sentences—long, convoluted, spiked with injunctions—where the end product would beautifully convey the intricacies of relationships and nuance of an idea in a relatively compact format. In English, my beautifully crafted compound sentences became run-on, unclear, unintelligible, fuzzy. These were the side comments in the margins that my professors in college and university would leave me. Often my heart sank or anger arose. I reread my sentences and they seemed very clear to me.
>
> So, I found myself, just like in high school, in the visiting hours of my professors advocating for my sentences and not for their content. Sometimes professors revised their judgment after reading my sentences three or four times over, and I was delighted. What I missed altogether though was that I needed to look at sentences and words very differently. In German, a sentence was a container within which a complex idea could be developed and shaped into a more coherent whole. In English, particularly the U.S. version, a sentence is only a component, and expressing it in its simplest, most accessible form is a hallmark of a good communicator. Complexity

was welcomed in German, a marker of good style, and signaled education and thoughtfulness. In my new language, complexity was shunned, and simplicity worshipped. Mind you, straightforward clarity is important in Germany in many aspects of day-to-day life, but not all. The nuanced world of thought and insight rendered clarity through complex sentence structures. . . . Every successful statement or bulleted list that starts with a verb that I write today is the product of a struggle with the English language that I fought out in many meetings or rewrites. I have accepted them as they seem to work. But, still and in secret, I like my compound nouns and complex sentences—a sort of *"Sprachvergnügen"* (the joy and excitement of language)—that I now nurture in silence.

As in this example, non-native speakers often come to English with an alternate conception of what it means to clearly communicate. Cognitively adopting the new rules for effective communication can be challenging, but sometimes even more difficult to process are the accompanying emotions: a sense of loss, including clarity of expression. As non-native English speakers adapt their habits to communicate with more clarity in English, they should understand that these feelings are not unusual.

Clarity makes it easy on our audience, as it reduces the effort they need to expend in understanding our ideas and us. When we are not clear in our spoken communication, they immediately let us know—by either telling us explicitly or signaling to us implicitly, with the look on their faces or an awkward pause. When we feel this disconnect, we easily panic and doubt our ability to recover and repair the connection. These moments of disconnect reduce confidence—in ourselves and in our abilities. The more frequently we panic, the more we feel derailed in our ability to communicate, connect, contribute, and excel. The erosion of confidence accelerates. Understanding the variables that govern the expectation of clarity by our audience is as critical as understanding, reversing, and/or preventing the erosion of confidence.

Of course, many native speakers also experience this vicious circle. For example, we work with people from the United States, the United Kingdom, and Canada who fear that they will become tongue-tied in high-pressure situations with multilingual audiences. Many senior leaders explain that controlling and overcoming their fear of stumbling, mumbling, and rambling helped them gain more connection and success. Leading in English across such diverse boundaries can derail even the most talented people, particularly early in their career development. Many international professionals feel stuck, with their careers stalled and their talent underestimated and underutilized as a result. Confidence and clarity are intricately connected and mutually dependent.

Let's examine several cases where a lack of confidence in clear speaking derailed two professionals, and a surplus of confidence saved another.

Jin-Young: Talent without Confidence

A talented young manager from Seoul—whom we will call Jin-Young—worked for a large multinational pharmaceutical company and was widely respected by everyone in the Seoul office. For his latest promotion, he was notified that he would be relocated to headquarters in Philadelphia. Deemed a high potential with a knack for innovative strategic thinking, Jin-Young displayed a quiet confidence that was well respected throughout the company. He was a good listener, contributed regularly to team meetings, and fostered positive relationships not only in his group but also throughout the company. While in South Korea, he communicated well with his U.S. and British counterparts. However, he had a secret. Jin-Young could not pronounce the name of his own company, which is loaded with "l" and "r" sounds. When he tried to pronounce it, people had a hard time distinguishing the name. At one point, a native speaker laughed out loud when he realized that the company name that Jin-Young was pronouncing was indeed where he worked. Jin-Young was embarrassed and devastated.

Upon learning that he was being relocated to the Philadelphia office, he became anxious about how well his English would be received. He had taken numerous language-training programs, including accent reduction sessions. Overall, his instructors gave high praise. His pronunciation—interpreted as his accent—was generally easy to understand, but the main trouble continued to be baseline "l" and "r" sounds. His private instructor drilled him for hours on these sounds, but Jin-Young only got more frustrated and more tongue-tied. He just couldn't say the name of the company with any clarity. He also began to question his overall communication abilities in English.

His confidence was low. Add that to the fact that he had never lived in an English-speaking country, and Jin-Young was nervous, apprehensive, and anxious. Upon arriving at the Philadelphia office, he decided to be humble and began speaking very softly, hoping that no one would hear his mistakes. Because of his low tones and timid approach to communication, he had a difficult time developing influence with senior managers, direct reports, and peers. The company had also recently been promoting executive presence as a key leadership attribute. He attended another accent reduction program, but he was clearly defeated and totally intimidated. The result was that Jin-Young returned early from a U.S. assignment that was widely viewed as a surprising failure in his promising career.

Edward: A Brooklyn Story

Edward, born and raised in Brooklyn, was a brilliant marketing software programmer, a leader in the field and widely recognized as a subject-matter expert at the multinational software giant where he worked. His native-speaking colleagues would often tell him to slow down when he spoke. Along with his classic Brooklyn accent, Edward not only mumbled but also faded at the end of his sentences. He started speaking with the best intentions but drifted inward by the end of his thoughts. It was almost as if he were speaking to himself. Edward might be described as the "absent-minded genius" who was often oblivious to others around him. Yet without question, his performance—mostly conducted behind his computer screen—was the best company-wide.

Edward was asked to go to London on a short-term assignment and teach a team of software programmers how to implement the latest updates to the newest marketing software. You would think—as the leaders at Edward's company did—that Edward would be able to overcome any communication issues since he was being sent to a native-speaking environment. Nothing could have been further from the truth. Edward was not well received by the London office. His sessions were described as "incomprehensible" since the British programmers did not understand most of what he said.

Edward left London feeling disgraced, and his confidence took a major hit. He would later describe the assignment as the most humiliating experience of his career. He never left the United States again.

However, something interesting and highly instructive happened when he left. The top programmer in the London office, Stephen, sat down to fully understand Edward's program. He took the course manual that Edward had provided and methodically went through the training on his own. Stephen found the manual to be impeccably developed, the logical flow of the instruction masterful, and the overall concepts the best he had ever seen. He realized Edward was a master of clarity in thought, but simply could not connect with his audience because of his lack of clarity in communication.

Pengfe: How to Build Confidence with Marginal English Skills

Pengfe, originally from China, had been living in San Francisco for almost 10 years. Working for a multinational banking conglomerate,

Pengfe was considered a subject-matter expert in futures and published numerous industry-leading articles on how Fortune 500 companies could minimize their risks by developing investing strategies around the futures markets. With a problem similar to that of Jin-Young, his lack of clarity in pronunciation caused him great stress when working with native-speaking colleagues—including external clients. But the more his esteem grew in the industry, the more people wanted to hear from Pengfe. While Jin-Young spoke in low tones to avoid having people hear his mistakes, Pengfe basically spoke in muddled and mumbled tones. The subconscious thought process was: "If no one can understand me, then no one can hear my mistakes." Mumbling became a habit, and he was especially challenged when delivering presentations or when speaking over the phone. Worst of all, each morning he was asked to speak on a microphone to the department to let them know the future outlook for that day.

Pengfe lacked confidence and know-how. He had particular problems with vowel patterns and—like Jin-Young—with "l" and "r" sounds. He took some private sessions with a voice coach, who immediately decided to convince Pengfe that his accent was just fine, and that he should not change it. Pengfe was intrigued. Furthermore, the coach worked with him on articulation, using vocal variety that helped create a range in his volume, intonation, and speed. Instead of endlessly drilling him to change sounds that were ingrained in his muscle memory, the coach helped him with a few work-arounds. For example, Pengfe could not pronounce the word *pool*, which is an important word in finance: "pool of investments" or "pooled funds." Pengfe—instead of avoiding the important term—was told to force his audience to understand it. One way would be to spell it out: "pooled funds—'pooled' is p-o-o-l-e-d—pooled funds." Another way was to create a reference, such as saying "pooled funds—you know, like a swimming pool of funds." Once the audience heard the reference, they understood the term Pengfe was using. Then he was coached to proceed in speaking with great confidence and deliberation—as if there was nothing wrong with just spelling out a word. His coworkers began to fully understand his morning messages, and the struggle with understanding Pengfe began to diminish. He still always fights a lack of clarity in his English, but he focuses on the audience and creates strategies to force their understanding.

Interestingly, Jin-Young was a better speaker of English than Pengfe. But Pengfe had success with English whereas Jin-Young and even Edward as a native speaker did not. The difference? Pengfe was not drilled endlessly on sounds that were impossible for him to make. Perhaps a work-around on the company name might have saved Jin-Young's international rotation. Pengfe was coached to build confidence, whereas Jin-Young felt that his English would only fail him.

Key Takeaways from Jin-Young, Edward, and Pengfe

What do Jin-Young's, Edward's, and Pengfe's stories illustrate? Their experiences help us extract the following insights:

- Confidence and clarity are intricately connected and mutually dependent.
- Perception of English impacts the audience's confidence in the speaker as well.
- Challenging sounds in English might be impossible for some people to make.
- Constant sound production drills might not work and could erode confidence.
- Creating work-arounds can force the listener to understand.*
- Enhancing articulation and strategic vocal variety helps.
- Proceeding with confidence is the most important element.

---

*You will find examples of work-arounds in the Toolkit.

Let's take a deeper look at work-arounds and reexamine Pierre's situation in Chapter 1. Traditional thinking leads us to the conclusion that the problem lies with Pierre. Since Pierre is the non-native speaker, he should strive to reduce his accent so that he could be better understood—in this case with the bartender. After all, the intended message should be the received message. If the purpose is to be understood, then the solution must be accent modification. However, the logic is flawed and creates a natural disconnect: many adults who did not attend school in an English-speaking environment cannot reduce their accents, regardless of their background and education.

If you are a non-native English speaker and you feel like you have hit a wall, you are not alone. If you are a native English speaker and can't relate to this, try living in another country and communicating in a different language. Could you do it? Even if you could, could you do it for a year, three years, a lifetime? When so much emphasis is placed on accent, you spend a lot of your day's energy thinking critically about your speech and your accent rather than about the tasks at hand. The valuable solution here is to identify what practical skills you must possess to be better understood with your accent, or when speaking with non-native English professionals.

The real-time, real-life solutions come from both sides of the communication cycle.

First, Pierre could have easily used a work-around—a strategy to force his listener to understand: "I want number 3 on your menu." He could have also said, "Don't overcook it," if the bartender could not understand "medium rare." English, as in any language, allows for multiple ways to say the same thing. However, in this case, both the native speaker and the non-native speaker got locked into patterns of communication as if they were married to them. We see this with public speakers who lose words, hesitate, and struggle to come up with something. They often have a "mini-meltdown," letting their audiences know that they are struggling: "Ugh, I can't think of that word" or "How frustrating—I am sorry."

A better strategy would be to stop looking for the word and say something like "Let me rephrase that" and then begin again. Versatility of expression provides great flexibility for both native and non-native speakers. (See the Toolkit for methods to improve versatility of expression.) Clearly, this solution is much easier for native speakers who grew up with the language and have a reservoir of words and phrases readily available. Pierre becomes fixated and wants the bartender to understand his English, so he tries again and again—using the same words—without any results. The added danger of proceeding with this type of communication is that the native speakers might infer that this particular communicator is not sharp, smart, or prepared. Perhaps this bias is unconscious, but either way, the result is the same. The non-native speaker is perceived to have inferior skills or ability and, as a result, feels substandard.

Let's not just single out Pierre for the problems in this interaction. "It takes two to tango," and the bartender could also have chosen a different approach and assumed some responsibility to make sure the intended message was the received message. Whether this particular communicator does not have the skills to be flexible or does not care to try makes a huge difference. Skills can be built, but apathy can only be a deterrent. The bartender had easy solutions for this communication problem. He could have asked Pierre to point at it on the menu, or could have offered up an opportunity for Pierre to rephrase his thoughts. Instead, the bartender simply blocked the message and was baffled.

What these cases illustrate is that clarity in English can be elusive and is all too common in organizations in which communication norms and cultural standards are dominated by native English speakers. As an international professional, you could be perceived by your team members or managers as lacking in clarity. Then you could be judged as deficient in those nebulous qualities we refer to as assertiveness, executive presence, or communication skills. Once that impression is formed and articulated, it is rarely challenged, and it can set in motion a potentially treacherous chain reaction.

In short, your accent is the problem, and it is yours alone. Or perhaps you are lacking in assertiveness, as Jin-Young was perceived. Thus, you should fix it with training. Then, perhaps the training company employs a junior-level coach who does not understand your pain in the business world. The training focuses on changing how you sound rather than how you could be understood. When you cannot easily change the sounds, the drilling becomes more intense. Your coach is well intentioned but can trigger a vicious circle of diminished confidence, poor performance, and loss of motivation that is associated with the phenomenon of the "stereotype threat."[2] It is important to understand how insidious this dynamic is and how easily it can be triggered, even for seasoned and seemingly successful people. As an example:

> We know one non-native speaker who has been living and working in the United States for more than 20 years. For that same amount of time, he has regularly facilitated and presented to clients in English. He is seasoned and generally exudes a high degree of confidence, but his confidence erodes when triggered by native speakers who talk quickly or expect him to converse in rapid-fire speech. Almost without fail, his confidence deteriorates with an intensity that does not seem to ease over time. As a listener, he panics when it becomes difficult for him to follow and understand. He tenses up and becomes extra vigilant, which stifles his own ability to concentrate, and he loses focus and finds it hard to respond effectively and intelligently. Hearing his own responses falling short of his own expectations, he flails even more, which further undermines his effectiveness. As a result, he avoids such intensely stressful interactions with fast talkers.
>
> However, that is not an effective strategy, particularly in New York City, where many of his clients are. In addition, there are frequently situations that trigger a similar erosive cycle, as it has become quite popular in conferences and meetings to "speed present"—to communicate in an accelerated fashion, compressing

the message into short three-, six-, or 10-minute segments. Naturally, the strategy (and expectation) for most presenters is to speak faster—and the more he tries, the more he flusters. His hands become clammy, he hears his accent get stronger, he searches for the right words, and he loses focus on the audience and his message. He has built himself some strategies to keep up the appearance of confidence—nonverbally—but he shrinks inside, and such stressful experiences generally end with an intense migraine.

We don't want to suggest that assertiveness training or accent modification training are not useful solutions. Either can add significant value under the right circumstances, but we want to caution against seeing them as default solutions, particularly when they can stifle rather than elevate talented people. We may need to challenge the assumptions we make when we are confronted with seemingly unclear communication and need to engage in meaningful changes that boost both confidence and clarity. This works when the environment is open, understanding, and supportive of the needs of international professionals. This includes a deeper appreciation of the challenges associated with accent and communication.

Examining Accent and Communication

Accent should perhaps be nothing more than an expression of our individuality—a sort of trademark as personal and unique as our signature. Henry Kissinger famously expressed this sentiment:

When I first came to this country, I was very conscious about my accent, but that was before I turned it into a trademark.

—Henry Kissinger[3]

Kissinger encapsulates a long and difficult inner process that starts with a form of self-consciousness that can easily create a distance—as nagging as it is intractable—from the larger social environment in which one is inevitably branded as a "foreigner."

Joerg experienced this firsthand at least twice. The first time happened during his perpetual struggle as a native German speaker living and working in the United States. The second time happened when he was teaching an accent reduction program at a local college. What qualified him was *not* the elimination of German traces in the way he speaks English, as that did not happen. Rather, he spent many years working consciously on the way he speaks English, which is now with a different accent than the one he came with. He struggled with the process and was no stranger to the self-consciousness that erodes confidence.

The accent reduction programs were always full, and the college needed to turn away applicants due to space constraints. There was obviously a demand. For Joerg, the first session of the accent reduction program was always the most enlightening and gratifying. He asked everyone to talk about why they chose this program, and the same types of stories were told repeatedly: participants came from all over the world and were in professional roles in various corporations. The average tenure was somewhere between 10 and 15 years, and the median age somewhere in the late thirties or beginning forties. They told of difficulties of adjusting to the workplace culture, feeling stuck in their careers, and struggling with building relationships and connecting at work. Most were clearly at a stage in their careers where functional expertise was no longer sufficient and relational skills were more critical to success.

But that alone could not explain why they chose an accent reduction program at a local college. The clue came from carefully listening to the stories they told. What brought them to the program was a treacherous self-diagnosis that goes something like this:

I have difficulties connecting and communicating; therefore, people don't understand me, and that must be related to my accent as the obvious

manifestation of my foreignness. If I just reduce my accent, I will be better
understood, I will feel more connected, and I can be more successful.

That this is a widespread phenomenon is supported by a study that found that speaking with a non-native accent was significantly associated with a feeling of less belonging, and this difference was mediated by perceived problems in communicating.[4]

Most interestingly, a few native speakers would also attend the program, stating they wanted to improve their overall communication. Some said they had a "New Jersey accent" and felt they could not advance in their careers, whereas others just wanted to be "more clear."

Some of the course participants could benefit from some form of accent reduction or modification—but that was never more than 10 percent of the full group. The overwhelming majority needed a different kind of help: they needed to understand their challenges differently, see beyond a narrow and negative notion of "accent," and transform their lack of confidence by actively building new skills. Their success was not predicated on erasing their unique accents, nor was it on blending into an amorphous mainstream held up as the more desirable and successful norm. They needed to learn what Bonnie St. John, the Paralympic medalist, said in a very different context: namely, that it took her a while to understand that "normal" does not mean "better" and that striving for "normal" will not lead to extraordinary results.

The "turning into a trademark" that Kissinger refers to has everything to do with embracing, cultivating, and leveraging our accents with confidence that serves as our source code for a more authentic connection and helps us thrive. When we find our authentic voice, our accent symbolizes our brand, signature, or trademark. We have turned the seeming disadvantage into an advantage. We have turned foreignness or otherness from stigma into asset.

Of course, this is easier said than done. After all, our accents tell a story whether we like it or not. They implicitly communicate to others who we are, where we are from, and where we belong. For each of us it invariably tells a story—native and non-native speakers alike. For example:

Carl, a university professor in the U.S. Northeast, tells the story of his accent with palpable embarrassment. He has worked hard to change the way he sounds. Having grown up in poor rural areas of Arkansas, he has been self-conscious of the prejudices that his accent evoked—a perception that he was uneducated and narrow-minded. These were not assets, especially in the academic world, and from early in his career he had received feedback from mentors that he should change the way he spoke if he wanted to get ahead. He worked hard at sounding more neutral, so that people could not easily tell where he grew up. He significantly attributes his success in the academic world to having avoided evoking stereotypes by masking his background that his natural way of speaking would reveal.

An accent can reveal our place of origin and evoke strong attitudes. As in Carl's case, a distinctive drawl can characterize a Southerner in the United States. When spoken in the South and with other Southerners, it affirms a shared identity; it says that "I, too, am from here!" Of course, that message would not reach the same depth of resonance as when it is sent among Southerners who happen to meet each other in the northeastern United States and who delight in meeting someone from home. Here, the shared accent may well be the catalyst of a relationship that is bound together by the mutual experience of now living and/or working away from home. For the Northerners, the same Southern drawl may trigger unfortunate stereotypes and associations due to the status of the accent on a hierarchy in which some accents are considered more pleasant, educated, and prestigious.

In a 2007 interview, Dennis Preston, professor of linguistics and languages at Michigan State University, explains:

[I]n attitude surveys all over the country, we find . . . that New York City and the American South have a tendency to be at the bottom of the prestige hierarchy, that is, when language correctness is considered. New England's very often at the top. . . .[5]

Another example is the recent explosion of British accents being used to pitch a variety of products in the United States and Canada. What is it that is so attractive about the British accent? It certainly provides an aura of education and sophistication. It also reminds us of Wimbledon, where one indulges in strawberries and cream. Advertisers find it sexy and attractive to viewers. The cadence and the rhythm are so distinctly different from American or Canadian English that the viewer finds the British accent refreshing. The workplace will carry those same symbolic codes, providing a clear advantage for the British working outside the United Kingdom. The accent tells a story before we even get to know or understand the skill set of the person using it. In essence, a powerful stereotype has been created around the mystique of the British accent. Compare that to how Edward from Brooklyn speaks and the impression he leaves on his audience. Even take Wendy, who has a mild but distinctly Chinese accent. She is being told to attend accent classes.

When native speakers communicate, they send a wealth of social information that is coded into the patterns of sound, rhythm, pitch, intonation, melody, and other small verbal habits that distinctively season the way we speak. We frequently rely on our audience's ability to decipher, resonate with, and respond to this code to get the intended message across and evoke the desired effect of our interaction—consciously or unconsciously.

This is why we might consciously or unconsciously modulate our accent depending on the situation we are in. How subtle this can be and how quickly this is noticed became very clear one day when Joerg's four-year-old daughter, Christina, called him at the office. As soon as he answered the phone, she said: "Oh, Papa, you have your work-voice on!" What she noticed was a profound reality in human interaction and communication—we accent ourselves differently depending on the situation and context. She experienced her father as different and distant and told him so, so that he could switch into another way of speaking that she clearly recognized as a proper expression of their father–daughter relationship.

Vince had a similar experience with his son, Alex. Having come home from teaching a two-day workshop on effective communication skills, Vince sat down with his family for dinner. During their conversations, Alex—at that time maybe 12 years old—said, "Hey, Dad, turn it off—we are not on CNN."

These are examples of "code-switching," a linguistic phenomenon that occurs when a speaker is "alternating between two or more languages or varieties of language in conversation" (Oxford English Dictionaries). Code-switching is often associated with multilinguals (i.e., speakers of more than one language), who may use elements of multiple languages when conversing. Some of these blends seem idiosyncratic, and others are becoming more widely recognized: Chinglish, Spanglish, and Hinglish are just a few examples.

For our purposes, it is useful not to tie the notion of code-switching too closely to the linguistic definition. We like the perspective offered by Gene Demby of NPR's Code Switch project, who looks at code-switching more broadly: "many of us subtly, reflexively change the way we express ourselves all the time. We are hopscotching between different cultural and linguistic spaces and different parts of our own identities—sometimes within a single interaction."[6]

Of course, it is not any different for non–native English speakers. The example of U.S. English only illustrates a universal phenomenon. A native German, French, Turkish, Russian, Mandarin, or Malayalam speaker can just as easily recognize small variations of accent in their language and associate it with important social information, stereotypes, and prestige value that impact perceptions, attitudes, and dispositions in social relationships.

Just like implicit associations tied to names, skin color, physical attractiveness, or other attributes,[7] the perceptions associated with accent affect human behavior. One compelling study conducted with native German speakers found a strong connection between "linguistic performance" (i.e., accent) and cooperation. In the study, individuals tended to cooperate significantly more often with those who also spoke with their own home accent (referred to as in-group members by the researchers) and were more likely to compete when matched with an accent speaker from outside of their home region (referred to as out-group members).

The researchers explain that their findings demonstrate that:

The perception of an out-group accent leads not only to social discrimination but also influences economic decisions. [. . .] This economic behavior is not necessarily attributable to the perception of a regional accent per se, but rather to the social rating of linguistic distance and the in-group/out-group perception it evokes.[8]

Accent indeed evokes strong emotional ties that can bias interactions and judgments. This phenomenon has been found early in childhood, where regional accents turn out to be significant dimensions of social preferences.[9]

This helps explain one international professional's experience, who put it as follows:

I live most of my life in English now . . . , and what that actually means, I have learned, is that I am really grieving a loss of home— of that time and place that shaped me and my mind, including my attachments to language and its expressive forms. Nowhere does that become more apparent as in the dialect and accent. This hit me recently in a surprising way: As I was working, I was listening in the background to a political talk show in my native language.

I do not remember the subject at all, but when one of the guests started to speak, I immediately felt a deep resonance in my gut, a big smile of joy came over me, and I immediately knew why I had been binge listening for all this time. There it was, that visceral connection to the place where I did not have to explain myself, where I was not somehow "different," where I belong, and where I am socially rooted—far beyond words. Ironically, though, that feeling was activated through words, but spoken in a peculiar dialect—an intonation, inflection, and melody—that places the speaker unmistakably in the very same soil of my own roots. That instant recognition made me tear up. The depth of my experience that surfaced in that moment when I recognized this daily disconnect came as a big surprise to me. I also understood why, whenever I travel back, I sometimes linger in stores just to hear people speak in this dialect. And, when I return my rental car at the airport, I hope for a small exchange with the attendant in this dialect that lets me savor the tacit understanding and connection until my next visit. . . . I do not experience this in English. I am immediately pegged as "not from here." Most of the time, I don't mind, but I still feel that I cannot fully express the way I look at things and the thoughts I have. English is functional, but it is limited and limiting—it is not the language of my heart or stomach.

The phenomenon of accent preference and its impact on attitudes and behavior is equally important when considering how native speakers perceive non-native accents. A study found this to be a widespread prejudice.[10] The study consisted of two experiments. In the first, participants were asked to evaluate job candidates for a middle-management marketing director position. They were given resumes and photos of candidates and asked to listen to audio recordings of the candidates ostensibly being interviewed for the job. The candidate profile was kept similar and the script for the interview was identical. The only difference was the accented speech. After listening to an interview, participants were asked to indicate whether they would recommend hiring this candidate. The results indicated that non-native-accented candidates were 16 percent less likely to be offered the job.

Similarly, in the second experiment, the researchers evaluated the degree to which non-native accents influenced the decision to fund tech entrepreneurs. They found that those with non-native accents were 23 percent less likely to receive investment funding than native-accented entrepreneurs. The researchers suggest that the larger, underlying issue is that non-native English speakers are significantly more likely to be considered lacking in "political skill," which comprises far more than effective communication. It is the ability to be perceptive and to influence others—increasingly important for building a successful career.

We cannot conclude our exploration of accent without considering the non-native speakers' perceptions and experiences of both native and non-native accents. These are the very people who find themselves in accent modification programs, or silently wish they could reduce or even eliminate their accents to connect better, more fully, and with confidence.

Phil is a native Chinese who came to the United States in his 20s for graduate studies (it was during these years that he adopted his English name). He joined a U.S. multinational and after a year was sent to Singapore, where he was instrumental in growing the business and establishing a strategically important hub for the company, which positioned itself for anticipated growth in Asia. His contributions were noticed, and when opportunities to enter the vast Chinese market opened, Phil was sent to establish a delivery network across this vast country. He met with government officials at national, regional, and local levels, and masterfully navigated the political and relational complexities necessary to succeed in this emerging market. He became the first country manager for China for the company.

Of course, his native Mandarin served him and his company well in China; he relied on his heavily accented English to communicate across the Asian region and certainly with U.S. headquarters. After several years as country manager, he was asked to take on a leadership role at U.S. headquarters, and there he experienced what one of the authors of the previously mentioned study identified as a "glass ceiling." If he was in China he was an asset, but at the U.S. head-quarters he saw his career stall and he felt socially isolated from his peers. For many personal reasons, he wanted to stay in the United States, so he tried for a few years to regain career momentum, but floundered. Increasingly, he lost confidence in himself. He ended up leaving the company and starting his own consulting practice.

But Phil's glass ceiling hovered over his new venture. Despite his experience, he found it difficult to engage U.S. clients. We worked with Phil on some occasions and experienced the disconnect firsthand. We selected him as part of a client-facing team where he presented information and conducted short training sessions. The client provided feedback that Phil was hard to understand and ineffective in his role. Even after Phil received extensive feedback and coaching, the client insisted that he be taken off the account. Phil was simultaneously both disheartened and relieved, as he felt the lack of traction every time he communicated with the client.

Phil ultimately returned to Singapore where his career had begun. He is still puzzled by his "American disaster," as he calls it. He finds it difficult to understand that the very accent that has never been an issue in Asia and with so many international professionals suddenly became a stumbling block for him among native English speakers. The erosion of confidence has taken its toll, and Phil is only slowly getting his career back on track.

In native-speaking environments, the non-native speakers cannot help but communicate their foreignness. They may be taken by surprise by the distancing effect, or be highly apprehensive about evoking undesirable perceptions and reactions. In either case, not only do careers get stifled and potentials go unrealized, but efficiency and productivity suffer as well.

Phil's experience illustrates a phenomenon that we have observed in a number of organizations, particularly in the professional service industry and where customer service is key. When an employee is perceived to have an "issue with accent," this perception is rarely critically examined and can set in motion an undesirable chain reaction. The idea of "accent" in such organizations carries the unconscious bias of signaling a perceived lack of executive presence, "polish" and/or communication skills, and therefore "risk." The impact is severe: the "accented individual" is underutilized, and the investment in his or her improvement decreases or, in the worst-case scenario, simply stops. Further, any development recommendations are often ineffective, mostly because the impression of "accent" has not been fully examined. In turn, opportunities are either limited or stifled, and in the absence of career progression the individual voluntarily or involuntarily leaves the organization. We call this *the "accent" trap* (see Figure 2.1).

We have observed the following breakdowns to significantly hinder the full utilization of international professionals:

- Inadequate or inaccurate understanding and diagnosis of the "accent" perception
- Ineffective and/or inaccurate feedback to the "accented" professional

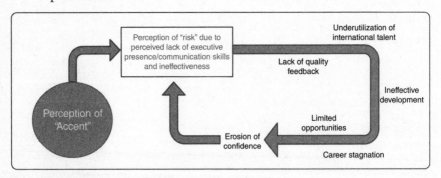

Figure 2.1   The "Accent" Trap

- Ineffective and/or wrong development solutions are being provided to the "accented" professional and/or his or her manager
- Insufficient attention to the role of managers/leaders to support and credentialize "accented" professionals

To avoid this trap, it is important that we deconstruct the impression of "having an accent," not linguistically, but in terms of the social context of work. In our experience with international professionals and their managers, we have learned that the impression of having an accent is most likely a composite of three factors: non-native pronunciation, non-native language use (including vocabulary), and differences in normative communication style (cultural style). The perception of the *risky* accented individual is heightened when he or she meets with customers, delivers critical presentations, provides business pitches, or builds rapport with key personnel. We call these "critical performance contexts," as they are critical to a business and generally associated with high risk and low tolerance for failure. In such situations, the impression of accent signals potential flaws and risk of non- or even substandard performance.

Now, only non-native pronunciation is a technical accent issue. Few managers are sufficiently skilled in assessing the situation around international professionals well, providing appropriate and useful feedback and then suggesting and supporting meaningful change. Figure 2.2 visually depicts the conditions and scenarios that yield beneficial outcomes for the individual and the organization. We hope this framework can serve as a tool for anyone who manages international professionals who find themselves worrying about optimizing the international workforce.

Native-speaking managers can help their organizations strengthen the talent pipeline by deconstructing the impression of accent and critically examining the degree to which true accent, language, culture, skill, and capability play a role. Only then can the appropriate

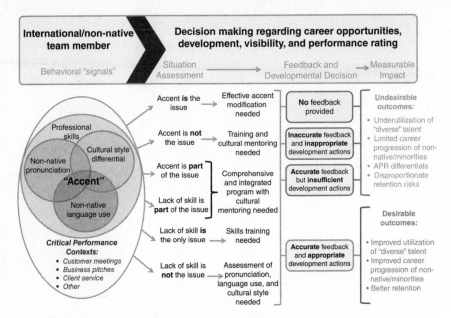

Figure 2.2   Analysis Framework

development solutions yield the desired outcomes. Providing meaningful, constructive, and situation-specific feedback makes the difference. Organizations seeking to harness the full power of their international talent will do well to train their managers and put in place evaluative frameworks and expectations to support accented professionals adequately. Such skills should build upon the general awareness and mindful use of English by native speakers in an international context. All too often, such awareness and sensitivity is lacking, as Ms. Singer Lee's experience illustrates. She adapted her name to English from her original name, Li Xing Ha, and works in the Chengdu (China) office of a large global manufacturing company. She was very confused about the communication style of many native English speakers in her organization. The e-mail read:

Dear Singer: I am coordinating the global inventory management project for the group. I am putting together a report in preparation for a global supply chain review meeting scheduled in two weeks. The SLT is trying to identify the low-hanging fruit in the optimization. Given that it is for the SLT, I do not want to cut corners and need a detailed logistics report from your operation—I understand you are the right person to contact. Can you tell me ASAP if you can:

1. Submit a full report and meet this aggressive deadline?
2. Make additional resources available other than your own sweat equity?
3. Submit it in final form? (I am worried about language—the report needs to be in English!)

I would very much appreciate your help on this—J

Singer added that the e-mail came from someone at headquarters, Joan, with whom she had never had any contact before. Most critically, she wanted advice on how to best respond, as she was confused and frustrated by this message. She mentioned that she did not know which "fruit" (the company manufactured machine parts) or "corners" Joan was talking about. She also did not understand the terms "sweat equity" and "ASAP." Beyond these idioms, she did not know what "final form" entailed. Singer was nervous about her English ability, particularly when it was meant for senior leaders. Overall, with less than two weeks before the deadline, and with little clarity on what she was being asked to do, Singer did not feel confident she could do a good job. As her team frequently received these type of communications, the frustration became only more widespread among them.

This case stands in for the experiences of many international professionals who are not using English as part of their global team relations. The lack of clarity is only aggravated by language aspects. Confusing global-matrix relationships, insufficient trust and interpersonal relationships, unclear expectations, and confusing language can easily compound and translate into daily patterns of frustrations that are not easily addressed. Clearer, more conscientious communication can go a long way to counteract the ambiguity embedded in the organizational context of global companies. As this case illustrates, native English speakers have a responsibility to reduce the lack of clarity created by insufficient explanation and expectation setting as well as the overuse of idiomatic expressions.

The propensity for informal communication in many native English-speaking work environments makes the use of idiomatic expressions a particularly vexing challenge. Consider, for example, the following message by a team leader to rally a globally distributed team in preparation for a particularly difficult year, given the financial crisis of 2008–2009:

> Team—Happy 2009! I was kicking around some ideas over the holidays and think we need a strategy meeting so that we can kick off the new year like white on rice. Given how things are shaping up, we can't afford to wait for the Hail Mary pass at the end of each quarter to make our numbers—we'll need to knock it out of the park every month.
>
> We've all had our holiday break and now it's time to get back in the saddle. So, let's have a kick-off meeting on Monday and blow the dust off and kick-ass this year!
>
> I want everyone to pitch in and dig deep and be prepared to discuss ways that you can start the ball rolling immediately. I need everyone's participation—this is no time to sit on the fence. Let's play this year like it's two minutes and counting.

In our experience, native English speakers—particularly in global organizations—often feel relieved that their native language is also the corporate language of international business. Therefore, they rarely work at modifying their communication habits, nor are they particularly aware of the derailers they introduce when communicating with their non-native-speaking colleagues. After all, in de facto terms, it is not native English that is the international language of business; based on the numbers of non-native English speakers, the norm is set by speakers of English as a foreign language.

This is rarely officially acknowledged or even leveraged. In our decade-long work in this area, we have found only one company that has declared its official language of global business to be "broken English." The impact of this declaration has been significant. It relieved everyone of the concern about the correctness of their English and focused on the efficiency of communication. Clarity of communication, after all, is not a function of correct grammar or spelling. Of course, it was not enough to just declare this standard; it needed to be explained by top leaders in the company. That most of the top leaders were non-native English speakers made this a very personal issue for them as well.

However, the relative disadvantage that non-native speakers have when communicating in a native-speaking environment is just one side of the coin. In a global context, where it is common for people from a wide variety of backgrounds to work together, non-native-accented English is the norm. In such a context, native speakers may be the ones at a disadvantage and require further skills. Even though it is not always easy for non-native speakers to understand each other, there is a shared difficulty of rendering thoughts and ideas in a language between them that is not experienced by native speakers. There is frequently more patience and forgiveness for technical mistakes; this shared sense of disadvantage can reduce if not fully eliminate accent as a potential source of both bias and inhibition. The shared bumpiness of needing to figure out how to best understand one another through deeper, conscious, and conscientious listening that prioritizes the quality of ideas over the technical quality of their spoken or written words is a uniting force.

This is powerfully illustrated by an experience shared with us by Katarzyna (Kasia), from Poland, and her colleague, Paula, from Scotland, who were both part of a global team made up of members from various countries, including the United States, Scotland, Sweden, Poland, the Netherlands, India, Egypt, and Turkey:

Kasia: I think it was really tough for the native English speakers on this team. Most of us were not native English speakers, and that was exactly what we had in common. And, somehow, we understood each other better than the native speakers. For example, I understood my colleagues from Turkey and Sweden so much better than those from Scotland and the United States. And it was not the speed, but the clarity. American English is hard to follow because it sounds like all the words are running together. And I really had a hard time following you at first, Paula—your Scottish accent is sometimes difficult to understand. Out of all the native speakers, our colleague from India was the easiest to understand.

Paula: I am glad we spoke about our communication as a team. It was a strange experience for me as well. There were moments when I had no idea what we were talking about. The non-native speakers seemed to understand each other, and we native speakers were lost. I observed that they have this ability to interpret each other and for each other; they listen differently and fill in gaps. We native speakers were just totally lost at times.

Kasia: I think that is true. When I listen to a non-native speaker, I immediately connect on the basis that we both struggle with expressing our ideas and explaining our perspectives well. I become very focused on following their thoughts and helping them in getting their thoughts out. I also know that I can ask people to repeat or say that I don't understand and it will be okay. Native speakers sometimes are very intimidating to me, and they use words or phrases that I often do not understand at all. And I don't want to ask and look stupid.

Paula: Actually, it can be quite intimidating for native speakers as well. For example, I know that our American colleague also has difficulties with the way I speak; he told me so. That was a surprise for many of the non-native speakers. And then we also often find it hard to understand Indian English; we actually never considered it native English at all.

Kasia: That was funny. When we spoke about it in our team, we all discovered that, and Raju was quite upset at first that you did not consider him a native speaker. I am so glad, though, that we discussed how we communicate and our difficulties with English as a team. I think it made us a better team. It was a turning point for all of us and helped tremendously in improving how we worked as a team.

Discussing communication and the relationship with English as part of a global team is, also anything but standard practice; however, it can deepen relationships and understanding among team members. It can also reduce anxiety and apprehension regarding language and communication that surely exist on all sides. Kasia and Paula's team, upon having such a conversation, agreed that when someone used a phrase or an idiomatic expression that the others were unfamiliar with, the others were empowered to stop the process. The person would explain the phrase, and everyone could learn and advance their English abilities together. This also boosted the sense of cohesion among the team and developed important habits of listening more attentively to one another, taking more deliberate and conscientious care of how team members express themselves, and helping one another to communicate clearly. These habits yielded benefits beyond the language, and led to an overall improvement of the sense of teamwork and the team's performance.

So, what should we make of these insights about accent and communication? Let's recap and turn to action:

- Accent is a powerful anchor of our social identity and communicates important social information about us.

- Accent is therefore subject to the powerful forces of social stigma, prejudice, and bias—for native and non-native speakers alike.
- The presence of a non-native accent likely lowers the perception of competence and possession of requisite political skills, thus reducing the chances of being selected for specific opportunities.
- The perceived or actual bias frequently leads to a lack of confidence and inhibition by the accented speaker; this can significantly impact performance and opportunities.
- The impression of accent in specific organizational contexts can lead to the accent trap, which can suboptimize development, utilization, and engagement of international professionals.
- Native speakers require specific sensitivity and skills to lead effectively in an environment where English is the dominant standard of communication.

When non-native speakers predominate, there is frequently more patience and forgiveness of technical mistakes; the shared sense of disadvantage can reduce if not fully eliminate accent as a potential source of both bias and inhibition.

Given the predominance of non-native speakers in the global workforce—now estimated at one billion—providing native and non-native speakers with awareness, encouragement, and skills to navigate this delicate subject is key. We have developed a four-step process: Assess It, Embrace It, Name It, Leverage It.

Assess It!

If you are self-conscious about your accent or suspect that your accent hinders your relationships and opportunities, and are considering accent modification, a professional assessment may be helpful. However, you may need to adjust your end goal. The objective should not be to sound as close to native speech as possible. Rather, you should strive to reduce any aspects of your accent or speech pattern that seriously impede your being understood. Besides being easier to achieve, it is the only reason that would ever warrant any accent modification work. If you decide on a professional assessment, be aware that most providers do not share this perspective. Many are incentivized to turn you into a client and may want to sell you long and expensive programs.

Embrace It!

Non-native and native speakers who are self-conscious about their accents should adopt Henry Kissinger as their role model and self-confidently embrace their accent as their distinctive trademark. *We cannot overemphasize the importance of this.* Turning self-consciousness into confidence is not an easy transformation at all. It takes deliberate attention and a diligent personal program.

Name It!

Address your sensitivity and their perception bias head-on. When presenting yourself, acknowledge your sensitivity and call out prevalent biases. You may say something like: "I know I have an accent, and you may think I am not as effective in pitching business. But I can be very convincing, as my track record shows." Or you may say, "You may think that because my accent reveals I did not grow up here that I do not know how to relate to our stakeholders. However, in my work history, I have always built strong relationships with people who were different from me." Sometimes it is enough to just name your self-consciousness, for example, "I know I have a strong accent, and I hope it does not get in your way to hear my message."

Leverage It!

As Paula and Kasia's team experience illustrates, the simple act of paying deliberate attention to sharing the experience with language and communication in English can be an important trigger to inspire attitudes and habits within a team that drive higher performance. Listening better, communicating more deliberately, helping and supporting one another—all these can be critical by-products of sharing vulnerabilities connected to language, cultivating norms that help everyone, and easing the subtle and not so subtle stress induced by a dominant English language norm.

Here are a few things to consider.

Native Speakers Are Subject to the Accent Trap, Too

As we have seen, native accent and speech are not necessarily advantages in a predominantly non-native-speaking environment. People with certain types of accents may be apprehensive in a native-speaking environment due to specific connotations. Stating your sensitivity and consciousness that you too have a strong accent is just as helpful as it is for non-native speakers. You can say things like: "I know my accent may be difficult to understand, so please do not hesitate to ask me to repeat," or "My Southern accent does not mean I am slow; many satisfied client can attest to my proactive handling of their concerns."

You Should Inoculate Your Decision Process

When making people decisions, particularly regarding promotions or career opportunities, you can inoculate your decision-making process against unintended and unconscious bias. Many organizations are now infusing their talent-management practice with interventions and adjustments to reduce biases by clearly outlining the decision criteria, observing the process, intervening when bias becomes evident, and raising sensitivity just before committees decide on hiring or promotions. This typically includes specific attention to biases based on gender or ethnic background. Accent needs to be added to the list of unconscious biases.

Interrupt the Vicious Circle of Confidence Erosion and Stifled Effectiveness

When you work in an environment where native and non-native speakers communicate with each other frequently, you may want to talk about their experience with language. Encourage an open dialogue, and adopt some guiding principles for effective communication that recognize and normalize the difficulties of native and non-native speakers alike.

These five additional tips for when someone tells you to "reduce your accent" work well for native and non-native speakers working across cultural and linguistic boundaries. Understand the difference between accent and clarity of speech. We know many people who have strong accents and are easy to understand and people with light accents who are difficult to understand.

Five Additional Tips

1. If you have a problem speaking clearly, focus on:
   - Articulation
   - Intonation
   - Pausing
   - Vocal variety
2. Determine where your pain points are:
   - On the phone
   - In presentations

- In facilitations
- During business meetings

3. Build your confidence by:
   - Stating where you are from
   - Creating work-arounds (see Chapter 3) for difficult sounds*
   - Modulating your volume
   - Trusting your business acumen

4. Strategically ask fast speakers to repeat themselves.

   We know that asking people to repeat themselves might seem like an indication that your English is not strong enough to listen and understand the first time. However, you must walk away with the intended message, so we suggest the following strategic tips:

   - With clients or superiors, "I want to make sure I understand all your points, so can you please go over that again?"
   - On the phone, "I'm taking notes, so could you please repeat that?"
   - At a business meeting: "Could you clarify that a bit more?"

   See Chapter 3 for additional tips for native speakers who use "Not a Care in the World" English (speak too quickly).

5. Video and audio record yourself to fully understand what your listeners hear.

   Be prepared to be shocked when you watch yourself: Most people say, "I can't believe that is what people see and hear when I am communicating," so watch it twice. Record yourself speaking aloud—perhaps choose some content on the Internet—and practice being understood clearly. Then read the same content a second time and practice speaking with passion (acting like you are the newscaster on the six o'clock news).

---

*If you cannot make the challenging "th" sounds (there are more than one), then use a work-around. As an example, one of our participants cannot say the number "33." It sounds like "dirty tree." So, we coach him to say, "33 as in the number after 32." Try not to drill too hard on difficult sounds (for non-native speakers).

We anchored the discussion about accent and communication around the basic requirement: clarity. However, throughout the chapter we indicated that clear communication is far more than just how you sound. The audience's perception of clarity creates the standard, but these prevailing "expectations"—often unconscious— are out of our direct control. For example:

- The standard: make the clear "th" sound so that "three" does not sound like "tree."
- The problem: I cannot make that sound and have spent many hours trying to do so.
- The result: frustration for both sender and receiver.

Or:

- The standard: a flat accent that is easy for all to understand—like a newscaster speaking to millions.
- The problem: I grew up in area where accents are not flat, and I do not have the verbal dexterity to adjust on demand.
- The result: frustration for both sender and receiver.

As we have seen, the implications run deep. The speaker can feel inadequate, and the sender is making assessments and judgments about the possible lack of competence and potential of the speaker.

What is the solution? Remember—it's about you! Confidence in yourself is where clarity begins. Confidence is often the proxy for competence. Taking pride in your cultural heritage and your linguistic background is a critical first step for your success. Next, a thorough understanding of others helps you to satisfy the requirements of any given context and adjust accordingly.

If it does take two to tango, then this chapter helps you adjust your dance moves so that you will be a fluid and confident partner. It's about you dancing your way to a place where your voice is heard and understood.

3 | Speaking with Impact—It's about Them

This chapter provides a practical and motivational guide for you as an international professional to deliver impactful messages in English across languages and cultures. An essential leadership attribute, strong speaking skills are critical in multilingual situations where ambiguity and misunderstandings are more the norm than the exception.

Impact begins with confidence. Through our experience in assessing thousands of international professionals, we have found that many of them devalue and underestimate their own abilities. You will learn to challenge your beliefs and perceptions about your current use of English across multiple languages—it is probably better than you think. You will also learn the key recovery skills to help you overcome awkward or embarrassing situations that serve to erode confidence. Further, we examine the various types of English that most people use every day that cause disconnections, misunderstandings, and frustrations. Most important, by implementing innovative learning solutions, you can make a lasting impact.

In the second chapter, we took a deep dive into why communicating clearly is about you. Embracing your accent and adjusting your preferred communication style are as essential to building confidence as the environment in which you do so. Further, analyzing your own abilities to speak clearly will lead to self-discovery and a practical learning plan. When delivering messages with impact, the key takeaways are quite different. The focus is on others rather than yourself. *It's not about me. It's about them.* By embracing this expression, you will begin to understand the methods that leaders use to create inspiration, influence, and guidance in the workplace. Far too often, international professionals worry about themselves in interactions and wonder:

- How do I sound?
- Should I slow down to be better understood?
- Should I explain that more thoroughly?
- Is my vocabulary strong enough?

These inward reflections, in themselves, are good questions. In Chapter 2, Speaking Clearly, we asked that you self-reflect and develop a learning plan to overcome the challenges that prevent you from being understood. While that inward journey of self-discovery serves your personal improvement plan, it does not help you deliver messages with impact. Here are some questions that may help you target your messages more directly to your audiences:

- What do they need from me?
- How can I be concise and organized, so that my message is clear?
- How can I package this message, so they best understand my key points?
- Why should they be listening to me?
- What do they need to remember in my message?

Structuring your message from an outward perspective begins the journey toward developing strong, impactful communication. As you will see from various examples that we use in this chapter, far too many international professionals worry about themselves and how they are perceived by native speakers or multilingual audiences. Remember, believe it in your core, and say it aloud if you must: "It's not about me—it's about them."

In this chapter, we will also discuss the innovative solutions that you can employ to improve your performance in English. They include:

- Debunking your belief system
- Building new skills
- Recovering from mistakes with confidence
- Creating strong connection and engagement

To help us frame these key learning points, we have identified six different types of English that people are using in a global context. You will note that our examples include both native and non-native speakers since both groups will benefit by learning the secrets and the power of connecting with global audiences.

Here are the six categories of English.

Non-Native Speakers

1. **"Safe" English** My entire life people have told me not to speak too quickly, so I speak slowly so everyone will understand me. I make sure my tone is even and my sounds are crystal clear. I rely on a small set of words because I know their meaning and use them correctly. I know some idioms and use the same ones all the time. I might say, "At the end of the day, it is what is."

   Results Native speakers find your messages boring. You use the dreaded monotone and seem to lack enthusiasm. People think your language skills are limited. They do not know the extent of your skills, so you might be told to take an advanced conversation class.

2. **"Must Speak Perfect" English**   I will lose face if I make mistakes, so I try not to speak too much. When I do, I calculate in my mind the grammar and the vocabulary before speaking. It is true that I hesitate quite a bit, but I am trying to get it right.

Results   Native speakers feel like you are passive and reticent about sharing important ideas. Your hesitation breaks the flow of your messages. You seem to lack passion for the topic. Since you do not speak very much, you might be asked to take an accent modification class to improve clarity. You may be a hidden asset in your company—a gem waiting to reveal itself.

Native Speakers

3. **"Not a Care in the World" English**   I don't consider that my audience may speak English as a second or third language. My rate of speech is fast, and I use idioms on the phone and in my e-mail messages without explaining what my idioms mean. I don't always speak clearly, because I am in a rush. Time is money. I have a type A personality, and others should keep up with me.

Results   Non-native speakers feel intimidated and have a hard time keeping up with the flow of any given communication. Their confidence dwindles. Only a non-native speaker would include this as a communication area that you might improve upon. Native speakers think you are doing just fine.

4. **"Second-Grade" English**   I am overly aware that my audience speaks English as a second or third language, so I slant my English to a level that is so simplistic that a small child would understand it. I speak slowly and loudly, the way, in the movie *Rush Hour*, Chris Tucker comically shouts loudly but slowly to Jackie Chan: "Do you understand the words that are coming out my mouth?"[1]

Results   Non-native speakers feel like you are speaking down to them. It fuels the overwhelming feeling of inadequacy that supports the stereotype that you are treating them as if they are not as intelligent as native speakers. No one tells you that you should find a balance in your English, so your listeners can both understand the message and feel valued at the same time. Further, your very sharp and bright listeners might make fun of you for thinking they cannot keep up.

Both Native and Non-Native Speakers

5. **"Fading, Fading, Gone" English**   I have the best intentions when delivering messages. When I speak, I become very introspective and think of so many different things I could say next. I have forgotten there is someone listening to me, so my volume and articulation drift toward the end of my message. By the time I finish, I am basically speaking to myself.

   Results   Everyone becomes frustrated because only half of the message is being received, and it appears disjointed and disorganized. Your audience either asks you to repeat yourself or totally zones out.

6. **"Impossible" English**   I mumble. Perhaps it is because I'd rather not have anyone hear my mistakes. If they can't understand me, well, then they can't hear the mistakes. Perhaps I lack confidence in my message. Perhaps I just don't know how to speak clearly. Perhaps I just want to be left alone, so I can get some work done.

   Results   You are not chosen to speak in public, lead meetings, or face clients. Your growth in the organization is limited.

Throughout the chapter, we use real-life stories to help connect you, our reader, with people in all walks of life.

Language Example 1: "Safe" English

> ### Alejandra Learns That "Safe" English Is Not Her Best English
>
> Alejandra, a human resources (HR) professional from Mexico who has lived and worked in Washington, D.C., for the past five

years, provides insight as to why an outward perspective is important. She has always felt that English would hold her back since she has—as she perceives—a strong accent and a limited vocabulary. However, she recently has been promoted to a senior-manager position in her accounting firm and is now leading a small team on an engagement with a Fortune 500 client. Prior to her promotion, she supplied her team with precise information regarding complex corporate tax issues. She became the go-to person for any of these complicated regulations. Alejandra, a self-proclaimed introvert, prefers the intimacy of private communication. People would call her by phone or come to her desk asking for her opinion and advice. She was always helpful and instructive. Noticing her work, the firm promoted her.

With the promotion came more complicated communication challenges: facilitating meetings, presenting proposed ideas to clients, and delivering feedback to her direct reports. She has an inherent fear of public speaking that stems from a bad experience she had—in Spanish—in the third grade when she froze on the stage and the teacher had to come out to help her. With her new responsibilities, Alejandra decided that "Safe English" should be her best approach. For almost her entire life, she has been told that she speaks too quickly. She wants to make sure that everyone understands every word. While she does not get overly nervous in private settings, she feels great insecurity and anxiety in front of groups. Alejandra is intelligent and knows that she must have an impact on her direct reports, the firm's partners, and, most important, her large-scale clients. She wonders:

- Can they understand me?
- Am I speaking loudly enough?

- Is my pronunciation clear enough?
- Should I slow down?
- Should I enunciate each word?
- Is my vocabulary strong enough?
- Am I making grammatical mistakes?

These are good questions to ask and answer. Self-reflection and improvement are always a part of a strong development plan. Speaking in English across different language bases can be discomforting for both native and non-native speakers. These are appropriate questions to ask after any given business communication. They help us to self-reflect and self-correct. Alejandra needed to change her mind-set from an inward to an outward perspective. Further, she needed to do this in her own unique voice. She did not need to magically become an extrovert or change her core style. We guided her to the work of Susan Cain and to her landmark book *Quiet: The Power of Introverts in a World That Can't Stop Talking*.[2]

How could Alejandra accomplish the task of creating an outward perspective when communicating? In a private coaching program, we asked her to challenge her own beliefs.

Debunk Your Belief System about English

We asked Alejandra:

Step 1: What Do You Believe About Your English?

Her first belief (very popular among non-native professionals): "I lack confidence because my English skills are not adequate." Notice that Alejandra expressed this belief in excellent English.

We asked her, "Why do you believe this?"

- "I have a limited vocabulary."
- "People have a hard time understanding my accent."
- "I only have mediocre communication skills."

Step 2: Is It True?

We assessed her English in two ways: First, we gave her a professional battery of performance exercises and evaluated them. Next, we informally interviewed several key colleagues, asking them about Alejandra's communication skills.

The results regarding Alejandra's English:

- True: She lacks confidence.
- False: Her English skills are not adequate.
- False: She has a limited vocabulary.
- False: People have a hard time understanding her because of her accent.
- Partially true: She has mediocre communication skills.

Step 3: What Are We Going to Do About Those Areas That Are True or Partially True?

Alejandra developed a comprehensive learning plan to enhance and highlight her totally underutilized skills to help her break free from "Safe" English. With guided practice, Alejandra learned new strategic communication skills that helped build her confidence. She pursued the following areas of development:

- Manage the presentation process (she took a solid three-day training program where she was videotaped three times delivering presentations).

- Increase her range of expression through guided, innovative activities.*
- Trust her current English and vocabulary.
- Adopt a long-range plan to increase her vocabulary.*

Alejandra, a great learner and a true leader, built her confidence. She refused to lose, shifted her mind-set, and liberated her fears by accepting that "it's not about me—it's about them." Why is that liberating? Well, to make that shift, Alejandra learned several important lessons. First, from the videotape of her performances she learned, "What I am feeling is not what the audience is seeing. When I lose my place and can't think of word, I am not in total panic; rather, I am in *temporary* panic and the audience does not know it."† That sense of temporary panic means that most people—if they present long enough—will lose their place and feel like the world is collapsing. The intrinsic knowledge that this feeling is temporary and will pass helps all presenters get through this challenge.

Alejandra began to ask different questions when communicating with her listeners:

- Who will be receiving my message?
- What is the context?
- Is it a phone conference, private face-to-face meeting, live business meeting, presentation, or other?
- What does the receiver need from me to best understand my intended message?
- How do I package my messages so they are crisp, clear, and understood?

The answers will change based on where, when, how, and to whom you are delivering this message. For example, if you are a native

---

* See the Toolkit for specific learning activities.
† See the Toolkit for strategies to recover from public-speaking nightmares.

speaker on a call with a group of Japanese managers in Tokyo, you might decide that they need you to slow the pace, be careful to avoid idioms, and send concise, pertinent messages that are easily interpreted. If you are a non-native speaker speaking to a group from the United States, you might decide they need you to use strong vocal variety by alternating your pace, adjusting your volume, varying your intonation, and framing your ideas.

By fully understanding the context of your situation, you can adjust your English to the needs of those with whom you are speaking.

Language Example 2: "Must Speak Perfect" English

A Story of Yoshi and Satoru

Yoshi, a Japanese native, is a senior vice president who works for a large insurance conglomerate and has a specialty in marketing life insurance products. He is now on a five-year rotation to London. His baseline English skills are solid, but he hates to make mistakes and feels like he loses credibility when he does so. Yoshi attended many English language conversation classes in Japan and has become quite proficient. He does make some modest grammatical mistakes but speaks clearly and is easy to understand. He often confuses pronouns; for example, he may say "he" when he means "she." Once when he made this mistake, a woman from the United States laughed. Perhaps the American woman was just being lighthearted, but Yoshi took it very personally. He wished that he had just stayed silent rather than having made such a blunder. Being perfect in English is important to him.

He feels that his vocabulary is substandard and believes— since he has never lived in an English-speaking country before— that his English will be subpar.

Further, he apologies for his "poor" English when he meets people for the first time. Even though he knows that his English is pretty good, he feels that beginning with humility can then enable him to build trusting relationships with his counterparts. Yoshi further hesitates before speaking and sometimes interrupts himself to make sure he is making strong and effective sentences.

Before arriving in the United Kingdom, Yoshi decided that he would cautiously interact with others and should not overstep his bounds. He will not have direct reports in London, but will rather continue to lead his global staff members, who are situated in seven different countries. He will have to deliver presentations to the UK marketing team and lead meetings about worldwide marketing strategies. Yoshi was extremely nervous about this prospect.

Yoshi's predecessor, Satoru, agreed to stay in the United Kingdom for a month to help Yoshi transition into his new assignment. Satoru is one of the most engaging executives we have ever met and was the perfect role model for Yoshi. He convinced Yoshi that there was no need to speak perfect English. You see, Satoru's English was close to being a train wreck. While in the United Kingdom, he made constant mistakes, was difficult to understand, and had a limited vocabulary. Oh, by the way, he is—still to this day—one of the most successful leaders in the company. He has an executive presence that is infectious. What is his secret for a successful stint in the United Kingdom? Confidence. He believes in his product, and he engages his listeners with charm and charisma. While on rotation, Satoru never apologized for his English, willingly repeated information, and used work-arounds to force understanding. He had a great sense of humor and developed rapport with all his colleagues. He refused to let his English get in the way.

In private, Satoru always bemoaned the fact that he did not speak better English. He took private coaching sessions the entire time he was in the United Kingdom. He did make progress in those sessions, which helped his confidence. However, he also knew that he made constant mistakes and was often looked at in a puzzled way when trying to convey a message.

Satoru did not always have such confidence. While in Japan, his first boss—Koichi—became his mentor and dear friend. Koichi taught Satoru that perfection in language is not more important than your passionate drive for the product you represent. The result is performance and accountability, which Koichi believed could be achieved by any group, in any language, in any country in the world. Satoru took the message to heart and lived by its principles. He focused on his audience, and although he knew they would be better served with stronger English skills on his part, he also knew that a relentless and inspiring drive for a worldwide increase in sales would be the key motivational and influential message. His messages had great impact even though his English skills were not perfect.

Satoru took Yoshi under his wing. He noted that Yoshi appeared shy and reticent. He also hesitated in key spots, which made him seem uncertain about his message. Satoru provided Yoshi with some great advice but also knew that Yoshi must be himself and proceed with his own set of unique skills. After all, Yoshi did not have that same robust, extroverted personality that Satoru possessed. Rather, Yoshi had a quiet passion, one that could be equally effective but was not yet realized. Plus, Yoshi had strong English skills that were not being utilized because of his pursuit of perfection. He lacked impact because his obsession with perfect English was about him, not his audience. His misconception was that his audience needed perfect English. The reality was that they needed passion and commitment.

Satoru recommended a professional coach to help build Yoshi's confidence. Yoshi came to New York for an intensive three-week engagement with our firm. We began by discovering and identifying Yoshi's strengths. Then we took him through some key items that he believed about himself and his communication skills.

Debunking Yoshi's Belief

Step 1: It Is Polite to Tell People My English Is Not So Good

After all, Yoshi is a non-native speaker and does not wish to appear arrogant. He does, however, communicate well in English.

Here are some possible results of underestimating your English when living in the United Kingdom:

- "Others think my English is not capable."
- "I am being chosen to take language classes."
- "I am not assertive."

Step 2: Is It True?

False: My English is not capable.   Yoshi actually has strong English skills supported by years of effective language training. He makes minor grammatical mistakes, but his listeners simply realize that he is not a native speaker, so the minor mistakes are no big deal.

True: I do not wish to be arrogant.   Yoshi's nature is to be polite and humble, and he should never change those core principles. However, the message being sent is that his "English is not capable." People in the United Kingdom and the United States might read this as an actual statement and not an expression of humility.

Step 3: What Should Yoshi Do?

> **Solution**   He needs to find a polite and humble way of letting people know that his English is more than capable.
>
> **Example**   "My English is not perfect, but I was fortunate to begin learning it in school when I was 10 years old."
>
> **Example**   When giving a presentation, he can say, "Thank you for accepting my content in English. Please let me know if you need me to clarify any key points."
>
> **Example**   The coach can advise Yoshi, "Simply do not apologize and do not refer to English at all. Proceed confidently and humbly with your message. This is not being arrogant."

Recovery Skills

Making mistakes in public evokes a feeling of inadequacy even for native speakers. However, that feeling is more intense for non-native speakers who experience insecurity about how they are being perceived. Yoshi is not alone. Many share these common reactions: the desire to hide, the intense anxiety, and the stress of freezing at crucial moments. The sinking feeling is that "I am failing in front of my superiors, my peers, or my direct reports."

The best advice that we can give to speakers when making mistakes in English is to follow a five-step process that will help them to maintain confidence:

1. Proceed with passion. Just because you made a mistake does not take away from the importance of your message.
2. Expect that you will make mistakes. By trying to speak perfect English, you are trying to do the impossible.
3. Acknowledge and embrace the anxiety—it never goes away, but you can learn to manage it.
4. Use effective techniques to manage the moments when you do make mistakes.

5. When the interaction is complete: recall the mistake, expand your self-knowledge, and try to improve. Then, move on with confidence.

Yoshi needs to learn that mistakes are inevitable. After all, this is his second language. Rather than staying silent, he must learn to recover.[*]

Example   The misuse of pronouns: "He [should be 'she'] said the reports are due by the end of week." Someone notices the mistake or Yoshi himself notices it, and Yoshi says, "Ah, I am sorry. I always confuse the pronouns."

Another example   Yoshi freezes when trying to think of a word or to phrase a concept. He tries unsuccessfully for a while and then feels like he is "losing face." Instead, he should abandon the search for the word or phrase, and tell the audience, "Excuse me, let me rephrase this," and begin again using different wording. Verbal dexterity will always be valued by the audience since they can imagine themselves losing a word in public.

Language Example 3: "Not a Care in the World" English

Samantha the HR Director and the Use of Idioms

Samantha, a bright HR executive with a great deal of international experience, loves to use idioms. She loves them so much that she does not even realize she is using them as they roll off her tongue. When with international groups, she usually assigns someone to point out when she uses an idiom, so she can explain it. In this case, she asked Vince to play that role for her. This setting was the company's large conference room, and the audience included about 15 native speakers and 20 people representing 13 different language groups.

---

[*] See the Toolkit for more on recovery skills.

She was delivering an easy-to-understand speech about the tasks that lay ahead for this global team. Her fluid style and measured tones were always well received with global groups. Further, she maintained an enthusiasm and a passion that sparked great interest from her audience. She said, "Now, before we throw the baby out with the bathwater, we should consider all of the options." I looked at the perplexed faces of the 20 non-native speakers, who all tilted their heads, smiled a bit, and were thinking: "Throwing away a baby? In bathwater?" Finding a polite time to interrupt, Vince raised his hand, and the HR director said with a smile, "Ah, Vince is going to point out one of my idioms." She realized immediately that the reference was to the baby and the bathwater. More than half of her audience did not understand the expression. But what happened next was revealing.

The audience members shifted their body language. They leaned in and grew extremely attentive. Even the native speakers were curious because even though this particular idiom is "old school," some had never heard it before. Samantha explained: "You see, when you brainstorm as much as we do here in the U.S., we become so comfortable in eliminating ideas. Sometimes, we might carelessly throw away a critical or important point. Thus, the cautionary tale is to make sure we do not throw out the essentials (the baby) with the disposables (the bathwater). It's really about streamlining and prioritizing."

The audience was enthralled. At break time, there was a buzz about the idiom and many of the non-native speakers were practicing it. This was the language they were missing, and they soaked up the new expression. Samantha had recognized this early in her career, and established a new standard and a new skill for communicating with audiences who speak a global English: idioms as bridge builders.

The standard solution that one hears for native speakers is to slow down, avoid idioms, and use a simplistic vocabulary. While we think that solution works best when on the telephone or when putting something in writing, we do not think it is appropriate when working with colleagues on an everyday basis. The key learning point there for native speakers is to embrace opportunities to help non-native speakers understand everyday language that defines our native styles. These non-native-speaking professionals have all learned English beginning with a textbook that includes:

"Hello. How are you? I am fine, thank you."

As a native speaker, when is the last time you spoke like that? How boring. Non-native speakers are hearing more of our everyday language. In the United States, for example, they might hear:

- Y'all doin' okay?
- Duh!
- Have a blast . . .
- Just holler!
- See you later, alligator.
- Cut a check
- Don't bark up the wrong tree.
- Here are my two cents . . .
- Let's pick the lowest-hanging fruit . . .
- We'll move the needle . . .

We need to seek opportunities where we can connect non-native speakers with everyday English. They value when someone takes the time to build a bridge that allows them a peek into what language structures make us native speakers.

Samantha is on the cutting edge of this principle and carefully includes her non-native-speaking audience by revealing insights into both language and culture. If she did not stop to explain her numerous idioms, then she would be speaking "Not a Care in the World" English. Rather, she uses language as a bridge builder. She cares for her audience and takes time to help them. The other idioms that she used during that speech included some interesting examples.

"Be careful not to cry wolf" is an idiom from one of Aesop's fables warning not to alarm for no reason. If you do that too often, then, when there is a reason, no one will listen.

"By the skin of their teeth" means the deadline was almost missed. The audience struggled with this one since teeth do not have skin.

"Let's hit the ground running" was an obvious one meaning the team should get off to a quick start.

"Play it by the book" means that the team should follow standard rules and regulations.

George, the Bank Vice President and Fastest Speaker on the Planet (Well, Maybe)

George does not have a care in the world when he speaks English. He is well spoken, has wonderful diction, and, for the most part, is articulate. George speaks quickly—very quickly. He has been told to slow down at times during his career in banking, but he feels that it reflects his type A personality, which works extremely well in the New York financial arena. "Everyone is in a hurry and they all understand me, so why should I slow down?" After years of working this way, speaking quickly has become his standard.

Of course, George may very well have great impact on his audience. His messages have zeal, they are targeted to his market, and he continues to prosper in his organization. Why should he change? After all, it's about them. . . .

Well, his audience had just changed. A group of six senior-level Chinese investment bankers were coming to George's group to provide expertise on target areas in China. Their English skills were strong; all of them had visited the United States before, but none had lived in an English-speaking country. George asked his administrative assistant to find out if the group would need an interpreter. He was relieved to find out that they wouldn't.

George called his meeting with the group to outline projects and define their responsibilities. He wanted to get everyone on the same page. The bank provided coffee and pastries for the morning meeting. Everyone was in a good mood, having been in good spirits and networking prior to the start of the meeting. George introduced himself, as did the other native speakers on the team. The conference room, with its view of the Manhattan skyline, was bright and sleek. The promise of success was in the air. Then, George started speaking at his typical pace, which was as fast as that of a racehorse trying to qualify for the Kentucky Derby. The Chinese bankers did not reveal any micro messages from their facial expressions. Another American in the room, Donna, noted that they must be good poker players.

Donna, who reported directly to George, knew that his rate of speech was too fast for the Chinese bankers to handle. She understood that their expressionless faces were hiding the fact they could not decipher what George was saying. She did not try to rescue the meeting, knowing that pointing anything out to George in public would be insulting. She was a master at career-survival skills.

After the meeting, everyone disbanded quickly to attend other meetings. The Chinese bankers were left alone in the conference room to discuss what had just transpired. In short, they were devastated. They did not discuss their direct feelings with each other, but they did feel a sense of dread for the upcoming project.

Later, in a private session, one of the bankers, Chao, told his coach that he thought after that particular meeting that coming to the United States was a mistake. He perhaps had overestimated his English skills, and that the bankers were going to be alone in their quest to provide solid information regarding the regulations of the Chinese market.

He felt that George would think they were not as bright or intelligent as their U.S. counterparts. He felt inadequate and not up to the task. The Chinese team was not expecting to be treated this way, but they were experiencing the stereotype threat that we discussed in Chapter 2.

Chao explained that the leader of his group, Shing, felt differently. He was very calm and told the group not to worry, and that all would fall into place. Shing then gave everyone initial tasks to complete to get everyone working. Privately, Chao wondered if Shing would be able to save the project, as the person who spoke English the worst was Shing.

Donna decided that she must do something to make sure that the Chinese team would be able to coordinate the work with George's team. She called a meeting with George to ask if she could play liaison with the Chinese team. She also wanted to point out to George that he was speaking so quickly that she doubted that the Chinese team understood much of what he said. She knew George well. He wanted people to be truthful even about his own performance. It was one of his best leadership traits.

George smiled when he heard Donna's comments. One side of him wanted to let Donna know that this was what he called the A to B industry—get to the point and get out. The other side knew she was spot-on. The Chinese do not speak English as a native language. In fact, he did not even take time to discover what limitations they may have. Perhaps making a stronger relationship with this new team might have served him well. George is notoriously task oriented and can often be seen as brisk and abrupt. However, he also craves success and in this case he knew adjustments needed to be made.

George assigned Donna to work closely with the team and help them understand the expectations. Shing was so pleased to find out that Donna was taking the time to work with them. Donna discovered that the team's English was pretty strong, but they were just not accustomed to rapid-fire speech.

Of course, good business sense saved the project during this example. "Not a Care in the World" English can cause significant problems if cooperative and collaborative participants are not in place. Often, someone like Donna is not there to help steer the boss, George, in the correct direction. The bank, in this case, believes in the motto: manage your manager. Further, a competent leader like Shing might not be there to calm down his team and lift their spirits. We provided this successful example to show you that miscommunication is not just a pure language issue but also a business problem deeply rooted in cultural and linguistic differences.

What can native speakers do to avoid using "Not a Care in the World" English?

- Recognize, respect, and respond to differences.
- Have a second set of eyes and ears to make sure the non-native speakers can keep up with the messaging.
- Slow down but maintain vocal variety to ensure enthusiasm.
- Create an additional feedback loop to make sure that all people are included equally in the essential threads of the message.
- Assign a liaison—a cultural interpreter to help non-native speakers understand expectations.

Language Example 4: "Second-Grade" English

"Second-Grade" English is almost the opposite of "Not a Care in the World" English. The speaker overcompensates for the non-native speaking audience by slowing down and using a simple vocabulary. The result may be that the audience feels like they are being treated like children and the message is degrading. Perhaps. However, many times the audience actually feels bemused and knows the speaker has missed the mark in gauging their ability to understand complex messages. While the intention is well focused on helping the listener understand, the opposite actually occurs. The speaker can lose the respect of the audience.

"Second-Grade" English

Consulting for a global pharmaceutical company, Vince delivered a U.S. cultural orientation program to a small group of French scientists to help them integrate with a U.S. team of scientists. Both sides consisted of seasoned professionals. The French scientists had fairly strong English skills—some better than others. The U.S. group had worked in France before, and some even had lived there for a few years. Their work together—while quite contentious regarding the science—never struggled because of language. Cultural differences about how they approached this project were evident from the first meeting. They battled through the work, but always maintained dignity and personal respect for one another. They enjoyed their dinners together and socialized with ease.

One day, all the scientists from both teams were asked to attend an early-morning team meeting with the marketing group to go over particular project details. The audience was quite diverse, with not only French speakers in the room, but also people from multiple linguistic backgrounds. Sophie, one of the French scientists, sat next to Vince. Drinking strong black coffee, they shared a few stories before the meeting began. When the meeting moderator started, he spoke ever so slowly thanking the international group for attending. He remained deliberate in both style and intonation. Sophie quietly groaned, "Oh, here we go again." Vince listened but stayed quiet the entire time, trying not to speak while the meeting was in progress. A few moments later, Sophie whispered, "He's treating us like children." No one except Vince could hear her. Once the meeting was fully under way, another speaker from the U.S. marketing team began her session of the meeting. Sophie again quietly said, "I bet she picks up the marker and writes it all down." Sure enough, the U.S. facilitator began to use the chart. Sophie, almost to herself, said, "I knew it—I'm back in school." The woman encouraged everyone to share and said, "Come on, everyone—there are no bad ideas." Sophie leaned in and said, "There are plenty of bad ideas, and she just wrote one down."

You could certainly argue that Sophie was being rude. She did not display her feelings publicly, nor did she ever complain about them to anyone else. However, her comments were revealing. Unlike Toshi in Chapter 1, Sophie did understand brainstorming; however, she simply did not like the process. She always felt like she was being treated like a child in U.S. meetings, and it began with the moderator using "Second-Grade" English. You should note that Sophie did not feel insulted, nor did she feel degraded. She simply thought the two native speakers were not sophisticated global communicators.

On the other hand, Sophie had no trouble communicating with the U.S. scientists, who knew that the French were strong communicators in English, understanding both the business and scientific terms as well as they did. The U.S. scientists also knew not to speak in rapid-fire phrases, so they could find a balance between "Second-Grade" and "Not a Care in the World" English.

From a linguistic standpoint, the French scientists were at a disadvantage with social English, never understanding the value of small talk or the colloquial expressions used daily. However, their hosts in the United States understood this and made them feel at home by including them in conversations and serving as their cultural translators while out to dinner. They also valued speakers slowing down on the phone without treating them as if they were not intelligent.

What are the characteristics of "Second-Grade" English?

- Simple vocabulary
- Slow speech patterns
- Monotone
- Condescending attitude (conscious or unconscious)

What can native speakers do to avoid using "Second-Grade" English?

- Understand that your audience is intelligent.
- Realize that most international professionals are proficient in English.
- Find a balance between not too rapid and not too slow when interacting in person.
- Use effective intonation as you would with native speakers.
- Use your normal vocabulary when interacting in person, and then explain difficult words or phrases.
- Check for understanding frequently.
- Ask if you are going too fast or too slow.

Language Example 5: "Fading, Fading, Gone" English

People who speak the "Fading, Fading, Gone" type of English usually begin a message with the best of intentions, but then get lost in their own thoughts, lower their volume, and stray from the original topic. As a result, their listeners struggle to grasp the message and will also fade out and think about the numerous things they need to accomplish. The speaker, the listener, and the content become disconnected.

We have seen this type of communication style often in participants who are in pursuit of lofty, intellectual goals that require a deep level of thinking. In search of occupational success, these professionals must explore wide boundaries, numerous theories, and volumes of research. When it comes time to deliver succinct messages, they are like—as the idiom goes—fish out of water. The challenge for these communicators is to connect their ideas to listeners who can then share their passion for any given topic. Scientists, mathematicians, information technology (IT) professionals, and university professors will often struggle making this connection. We can relate to the many professors we had in college who had little or no instructional skills. They were chosen for their brilliance in an academic area, but not all of them could transfer that brilliance into an instructional mind-set where they could have an impact on their students' lives. Think of the challenge that Dr. John Nash, as represented in the movie *A Beautiful Mind*, has when he wants to become more mainstream by teaching as a professor at Princeton University. The director of the department quips to the brilliant Nash that the first class he teaches will be the first class he ever attended.[3]

What are the characteristics of "Fading, Fading, Gone" English?

- Volume fades toward the end of a message.
- Reflection is inward, forgetting that "it's about them."
- The message becomes convoluted.
- The listener is an afterthought.

What can native and non-native speakers do to avoid using "Fading, Fading, Gone" English?

- Keep volume up throughout the message.
- Stay close to the value proposition: Why should people be listening?
- Maintain the conscious competent level: the listener does not know what you know.

Language Example 6: "Impossible" English

Mumbling is a problem for any speaker in any language. In fact, some international professionals are not very clear in their own native language. The problem is exacerbated when these professionals begin working across languages and cultures.

"Impossible" English

As an example, one Mandarin speaker, from a large insurance conglomerate in the United States, struggled terribly in an accent modification program. He tried so hard to make the difficult sounds in English and put it all together into coherent speech patterns; however, the training did not take. He fondly tells the story of how his instructor, a conscientious young woman, finally threw her hands up in the air and asked: "How well are you understood in Mandarin?" He replied, "No one understands me in that language, either." Stunned, she replied, "Why didn't you tell me?" Wryly, he said simply, "You never asked."

A key principle is uncovered in that example. Speaking English without clarity may have more to do with mumbling than it does with accent. Of course, it is doubly difficult to ask people to be understood in a second language when they do not speak clearly in their native language. Correctly assessing a mumbling problem can be tricky. The most important question is to ask if the individual has ever been diagnosed with a speech disorder. If the answer is no, then the next obvious question is: Could there nevertheless be a speech disorder? That assessment should be made by speech pathologist. For our purposes in *Leading in English*, we concentrate on those individuals who do not have speech disorders but have a hard time being understood.

Oftentimes, the problem for mumblers is that they do not know they are being unclear. The speaker cannot hear the problem and then wonders why the audience does not understand. "Perhaps it is more their listening skills than my speaking ability." Their level of frustration grows when people consistently ask, "Could you say that again?" People who mumble often struggle to get their careers on track because they are rarely chosen for public speaking, including facing both internal and external clients. In the intense search for talent in organizations, we cannot afford to leave people behind and disregard them. Why? Well, those people who do not speak clearly could actually be the brightest and the best talent in the organization. How would you know? If we follow the central theme of the book that "it takes two to tango" and the thrust of this chapter—"it's not about me; it's about them"—then we need to provide a substantial learning strategy for the mumbler to improve. What can be done for you or your colleagues who speak "Impossible" English? First look at the characteristics and then the tips on how to improve.

What are the characteristics of "Impossible" English?

- Lacks clarity of speech.
- Speaks in low volumes.
- Avoids having people hear grammatical mistakes by intentionally speaking quickly.
- Lacks pausing and avoids silence.
- Uses a lot of fillers: "um," "okay," "right," "like" . . .

What can native and non-native speakers do to avoid using "Impossible" English?

- Sharpen overall articulation.
- Practice diction.
- Use effective pauses.
- Learn to frame ideas.
- Increase volume using 1, 2, 3 exercise scale.*
- Read aloud regularly for the purpose of being understood.*
- Use effective intonation to emphasize ideas.

Connection to the Audience

The final part of our chapter on speaking with impact focuses on two key leadership attributes that you need with people in all phases of your life: connection and engagement. You will note that our lounge characters are struggling to make those connections, without which they are prevented from being impactful communicators. The stories they share reflect those challenges, and you get the sense that they will all find ways to overcome their specific situations. Good leaders do that. Influencing, motivating, and inspiring others all come from your ability to connect with those around you. As a leader, you need to make those connections to have an impact on your organization, on your superiors, on your peers, and on your direct reports.

In each of the six language categories that we outlined earlier in the chapter, you could see where the challenges in English could prevent impactful communication. With the proper strategies, you can easily and naturally create a flow that links sender, message, and

---

*See the Toolkit for explanations and exercises.

R.A.P.

Effective communicators naturally create a flow that links communicator, message, and audience.

Learn to RAP by recognizing, affirming, and participating.

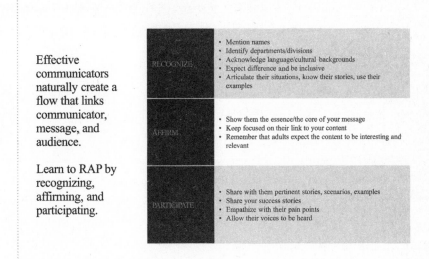

RECOGNIZE
- Mention names
- Identify departments/divisions
- Acknowledge language/cultural backgrounds
- Expect difference and be inclusive
- Articulate their situations, know their stories, use their examples

AFFIRM
- Show them the essence/the core of your message
- Keep focused on their link to your content
- Remember that adults expect the content to be interesting and relevant

PARTICIPATE
- Share with them pertinent stories, scenarios, examples
- Share your success stories
- Empathize with their pain points
- Allow their voices to be heard

Figure 3.1   Recognize, Affirm, and Participate

audience. Many international professionals experience high levels of anxiety with the thought of delivering any form of public speaking in English. You can use the following strategies to create a powerful connection when you find yourself speaking in front of any particular size group.

Begin by recognizing your listeners and using their names, then affirm why they should be listening to your message, and finally be sure to give them time to respond and participate. We call this the RAP method: Recognize, Affirm, and Participate (see Figure 3.1).

We recently worked with a professional from Nigeria, Adimabua, who spoke both English and Igbo as native languages. He was living and working on the West Coast of the United States, and many of his coworkers described his English as impossible to understand. They struggled to understand Adimabua's accent, and he tended to speak at such a low volume that people thought he was mumbling. The good news is that he works for a firm that values an inclusive work environment and recently has been promoted to manager. He also has been chosen to face clients who recognize him as an expert in banking law. Both his firm and his client believe it takes two to tango, and that talent is not based on how you sound.

What really gave Adimabua a problem was that he was asked to be the best man at his friend's wedding where over 700 people would be in attendance. It was to be quite a spectacular event—very formal, very prestigious. Adimabua was panicked. However, we practiced the RAP method, and applied its principles to help him develop his speech.

He opened by recognizing and honoring the families of the bride and groom, the families of the friends close to the bride and groom, his own mother and father, and the various regions from which people had traveled. He went on to affirm why everyone had come to this marvelous gathering, told rich stories about how he and the groom had caused some mischief when they were younger, and about how his friend's life had changed forever when he met his future bride. Finally, he asked everyone to stand and participate in this joyous occasion by toasting, celebrating, and sharing in the love that was so clearly in the air. He recognized them, affirmed why they were there, and asked them to participate in the celebration. He sat down exhausted, sweating profusely. Later, he described it as one of the proudest moments of his life.

The model works—even in one-on-one conversations. You see that Adimabua used the RAP model to ensure that this message was not about him but rather about the bride, the groom, and the audience. Because he did that, everyone came up to Adimabua to congratulate him on such a heartfelt speech. Now, that is connection. That is impact.

Another method to establish and deepen connection is impactful listening and influential linking (see Figure 3.2). Professionals create an atmosphere of trust, so people are comfortable in sharing information. Listening skills and connecting language are the key ingredients that help connect a person to the audience.

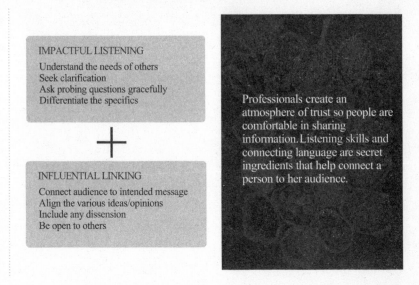

IMPACTFUL LISTENING
Understand the needs of others
Seek clarification
Ask probing questions gracefully
Differentiate the specifics

+

INFLUENTIAL LINKING
Connect audience to intended message
Align the various ideas/opinions
Include any dissension
Be open to others

Professionals create an atmosphere of trust so people are comfortable in sharing information. Listening skills and connecting language are secret ingredients that help connect a person to her audience.

Figure 3.2   Impactful Listening and Influential Linking

Let's use an example to demonstrate the skills here.

Pedro, a native of Mexico, works in Montreal for a large shoe manufacturer. He is the only native Spanish speaker in the compliance department, does well as a newly promoted manager, and has a wonderful reputation in the company. He was told that he speaks "Safe English" and should learn to show more passion in his messages. The other areas of his English are flawless. He responded quite well to coaching because his expressiveness in Spanish is robust, and he simply needed to emulate that in English. The skills were already there. Pedro has a secret weapon in his communication arsenal. He listens intently, and then threads and ties his message to his listeners. Here's an example.

His boss's boss, a Canadian senior VP, was wondering why the department had such a negative reputation throughout the firm, and she engaged Pedro in a conversation about it. Pedro knew his own boss would be comfortable with this interaction. At first Pedro listened. He then asked the VP, "Do other compliance departments have such challenges?" She thought about that. He remained quiet, patiently waiting for her response. She agreed that there is a universal negative feeling about compliance departments. "Hmm, I wonder—why is that?" Pedro asked. Again, she responded. It was at this moment that Pedro knew he had to share his own thoughts. Too many questions might seem like he was reluctant to share ideas with a senior-level executive. He said, "I know that branding or rebranding is now catching a lot of attention in the market. I just read an article about it. I can send that to you, if you'd like." She was thrilled and told him, "Please do so. Also, let's keep this dialogue going. I think we may be able to change a few things here." Pedro said, "Sounds great. Thanks so much for sharing."

Pedro not only listened actively, but also listened for impact. Finally, he tied the conversation together and created the best kind of influence possible—influencing without authority. You can refer to the Toolkit for the type of language you can use when you are using impactful listening and influential linking.

Finally, synchronize and structure your messages—whether you are in private or public conversation—so that they follow the classic paradigm: strong openings, relevant examples, and powerful conclusions (see Figure 3.3).

Your listeners will resonate with you and your message—especially if you deliver using concise structures.

Our final example in the chapter centers on Raj, an executive from India who works in Australia.

Raj is a senior VP from India who works for a multinational fragrance company located in Australia. He has been told numerous times to reduce his accent so that everyone could understand him. Two things became apparent: first, he could not change the way he

DELIVER THE MESSAGE

SYNCHRONIZE

STRONG OPENINGS
• Clear focus
• Memorable examples

RELEVANCE
• Topic directed to audience
• Strong, updated scenarios
• Attention getting

STRONG CONCLUSIONS
• Value proposition now has clear meaning
• Audience expectations delineated

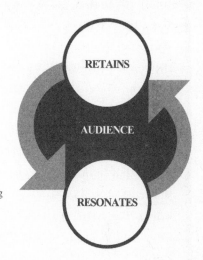

Figure 3.3   Deliver the Message

sounded, no matter how hard he tried. Second, he did not care to try. He quietly resented the idea that he was hard to understand since he had grown up and spent most of his life speaking English, especially at school. Further, he had been working in English his entire adult life and could not even attempt to work in his native language, Hindi. But Raj did respond well to the idea of delivering his messages with impact.

In strategic situations, he focused on beginning with a strong opening. The key learning point here was to make his point in a brief and concise manner. In a business meeting regarding the possibility of the company spending hundreds of thousands of dollars on a new software program, Raj began:

"I walked by a colleague who was working at his desk, and noticed that he changed screens and seemed annoyed. I asked him what was going on, and he said to me: 'This old software program takes me about five to six minutes to complete this task. I must switch screens three times.' My goodness, the new software program would take 30 seconds."

Note that Raj did not just open by saying, "We need a new software program." Then his audience would think: "Raj thinks we need the new software program." Instead, he started with a story that began the process of getting the audience to think: "We need a new software program."

Then he discussed the benefits and the relevance of how this software change would benefit the company. His audience was engaged. Finally, he provided a short and succinct financial analysis that his audience fully expected. He took less than five minutes of meeting time. His message resonated with the audience, and they retained the visual image of the employee struggling with the old software package. Rather than telling them what they needed, Raj showed them so they could retain and remember his very powerful comments. By the way, no one noticed his accent, but everyone saw an emerging leader.

Speaking with impact is like a glass and the water it holds. Which is more important? Clearly, the water hydrates us and keeps us alive. We cannot live without it. In this analogy, the water serves as the ideas that flow from your inner passions that you want to express to others. The ideas are yours, serving as your personal reservoir, a body of water that uniquely announces, "This is who I am and what I stand for." The glass, while of lesser value, holds that water and allows us to access it, so we can stream our passions and express our values to the world around us. Without the glass, we cannot hold the water. Without the water, we are nothing. This chapter is about the glass. You have the water, and only you can shape those inner passions.

When we say that "it's not about you; it's about them," what we want is for you to be the conduit that seamlessly streams and connects your message to your audience. When communication is working at its best, then the three elements—speaker, listener, and content—are all connected as if they were one. That is why you enjoy a great book. That is why you value any particular presentation: it resonates with you. That is why you love a particular film: it strikes a chord inside you. When you deliver a message, then you are the author, the presenter, the filmmaker. Your job is to make that message resonate. You are bringing your audience into your world, into your ideas, and into your authentic self. How do you do that? You focus on them. This chapter provides the structure for the glass to hold the water.

4

Developing a Compelling Narrative—It's about Moving Them

That is the hallmark of a rock and roll band: the narrative you tell together is bigger than anyone could have told on their own.

—Bruce Springsteen[1]

In Chapter 2, we spoke about the importance of turning "foreignness" or "otherness" from stigma into asset. We identified some important shifts in our attitude, mind-set, and skills that can boost confidence. In Chapter 3, we focused on the personal effectiveness that people must have to speak with impact. In this chapter, we will introduce additional insights that help you navigate the difficult intersection of language, culture, and success when leading in English. It takes us beyond the focus on language and clear communication with our audience ("them") and into the realm of culture and leadership—to the art and science of "moving them."

This is our short definition of leadership—a dynamic process of influencing that can be observed among members of a group and whereby the motivations, perceptions, and behaviors of members of a group converge and become transformed.[2]

In this dynamic process, narratives, or stories, play a central role. The insights about the art and science of the narrative are important for any leader, but there may be additional challenges for you as an international professional. As a foreigner on less familiar social terrain, you navigate the tension between your conditioned self (how you are expected and taught to be in your native environment) and your authentic self (how you truly are or aspire to be) in a non-native vernacular, English. As a leader, you will be called upon to transform the conditioned into the authentic self of others.

In this chapter, we hope to expand your appreciation for the role and power of stories to this challenge of leadership. We will briefly review key insights about stories and discover together why it is important for you to (1) know, define, and embody your story; (2) share your story memorably; and (3) weave a co-created and compelling narrative that moves others. Along the way we will provide practical points that will help you turn general ideas into practical improvements in your leadership practice.

Behold: The Power of Stories

Of late, storytelling has been emphasized as a key leadership skill, alongside strategic thinking, business acumen, emotional intelligence, and many others. Leaders spend considerable time and effort learning the technique of storytelling. Have you ever wondered why and perhaps how storytelling relates to the unique challenges and opportunities you face as an international professional?

In our experience, international professionals tend to feel at a disadvantage when it comes to creating authentic connections and shaping or co-creating a shared story and identity. Non-natives tend to encounter hurdles that native leaders don't face to the same degree, because they start off with less developed social connectedness in comparison to what they experienced in their native or home environment. However, this perceived disadvantage can also become a great asset—and become a compelling story in itself.

Stories across cultures are the fundamental building blocks of human motivation, behavior, and the choices that we make. Stories affirm our identity, explain our motivations and desires, and render our complex world and experiences coherent and intelligible. We need stories to define and to compel action. The specific stories we tell, however, are the sticky glue, the tissue that connects us in specific social contexts. For the most part, international professionals start outside of these contexts and seek a way to get inside—a path that comes with tremendous hurdles.

Before the invention and subsequent proliferation of writing, some 5,000 to 6,000 years ago, humans passed on knowledge through the oral tradition of storytelling. The human brain is wired for stories, as they capture and embody the fullness of the human experience, the connection between our inner and outer worlds. Beyond mere information, stories engage the full registry of our emotions and reinforce our social relationships. In that sense, stories are primal, and that's perhaps why they are everywhere. We just need to see them and understand what they do for us. Let's look.

We can see the fundamental power of stories perhaps most clearly in our children—they crave stories; they imitate and become the main characters; they replay, reframe, and iterate on the stories that surround them in the games that they play and invent. Children move in and out of various story lines seamlessly, connecting their story worlds with the supposedly real world, seamlessly combining and recombining the two in new and innovative ways. The games they invent and play are interactively improvised, co-created stories.

We preserve and evolve this fundamental craving for stories in our adolescent and adult selves, where it only proliferates and evolves into new forms, from our modern fantasy football, gaming, and binge watching of TV serials to our more conventional theater, TV, movie, and book consumption. Entire industries are built on our penchant for stories and narratives.

In 2015, the size of the gaming industry was expected to grow from just over $90 billion worldwide to $107 billion in 2017 with a steady growth rate thereafter.[3] In 2016, the television and video industry was a $280 billion industry worldwide. The global box office revenue of over $36 billion in 2016 is expected to grow to approximately $50 billion in 2020. In addition, the global book market was estimated at 114 billion euros in 2015.[4]

Neurobiology can tell us why stories are such good business. Paul Zak, a professor at Claremont Graduate University, in a *Harvard Business Review* article, explains that:

> a story must first sustain attention—a scarce resource in the brain—by developing tension during the narrative. If the story can create that tension then it is likely that attentive viewers/listeners will come to share the emotions of the characters in it, and after it ends, likely to continue mimicking the feelings and behaviors of those characters. This explains the feeling of dominance you have after James Bond saves the world, and your motivation to work out after watching the Spartans fight in *300*.[5]

We sometimes glimpse this transformative power when we leave a movie theater after experiencing a particularly gripping and engaging story. For a few moments, we may struggle to reconcile the world we were just made part of with our old, rather mundane reality.

Perhaps this is why across cultures and societies we revere actors, musicians, and artists. Their craft brings the innermost, subjective worlds of others to us, evoking compassion and emotional resonance. They interpret our world, connect us to the worlds of others, and tap our imaginations to envision a different, better, and alternative version of ourselves.

As social beings, we *existentially* rely on our capacity to share the emotions and experiences of others (i.e., empathy). Far from being soft or squishy, empathy allows us to understand how others are likely to experience, understand, and react to a given situation, to *collectively* respond in ways that secure our survival, adapt to changing circumstances, and thrive.[6]

Zak's research has demonstrated how much more effective and motivating it is to describe the challenging experiences of real people (including their names and circumstances) and how an action, solution, decision, or service could address the challenge and help improve their lives:

> Make your people empathize with the pain the customer experienced and they will also feel the pleasure of its resolution—all the more if some heroics went into reducing suffering or struggle, or producing joy.[7]

Joseph Campbell famously described the universal template, or monomyth, as an archetypal structure by which the social power of a narrative is unlocked. It exists within a myriad of plots, their variation and iterations streaming across communities, societies, and groups of various sizes. This monomyth is commonly referred to as "the hero's journey," which Campbell summarizes as follows:

> A hero ventures forth from the world of common day into a region of supernatural wonder: fabulous forces are there encountered and a decisive victory is won: the hero comes back from this mysterious adventure with the power to bestow boons on his fellow man.[8]

Campbell discerned distinct stages within three acts that form the essential structure of compelling stories. The structure roughly conforms to the following pattern. In act one, the heroes are part of the ordinary, familiar world; that is, they are like us. They receive a call to action or adventure, which they know they must accept, but fears and doubts hold them back. They seek advice from a mentor and receive something they desperately need: confidence, skills, clarity, focus—just what they must have to overcome their doubts and fears and embark on their journey.

In act two, the heroes cross into a special world and embark on the adventure/journey. They are now in unfamiliar territory, yet committed to carry on. They encounter obstacles and meet allies and enemies that slowly prepare them to encounter and withstand even more demanding challenges. They arrive at the most challenging point—often a specific location—that holds the biggest danger and triggers their deepest fears and insecurities again. They prepare for the biggest ordeal—a battle of sorts—that requires a heroic effort and profoundly transforms them. There is frequently a sense of "death," or loss from which the heroes emerge as stronger or wiser, endowed with special knowledge, insights, or capabilities of great importance.

In the third act, the heroes heed the call to return to the ordinary world, out of duty, the pursuit of a higher purpose, or to vindicate or exonerate themselves. On the way home they are confronted with their most dangerous encounter, for failure here is associated with far-reaching consequences. The heroes finally succeed and emerge victorious and reborn, now able to return home—transformed and endowed with special powers that bring hope, change, and solutions to the world they had left behind.

It would not be a surprise if this plotline reminded you of your favorite movies or books. Epic and generation-defining stories tend to conform to this pattern—from *Moby-Dick* and *The Catcher in the Rye* to *The Lord of the Rings*, *Star Wars*, and *Harry Potter*. The same pattern is also reflected and embedded in the many mythologies, spiritual traditions, and historical narratives that define societies, communities, and entire civilizations.

We create, tell, and respond to hero stories because they affirm our common humanity. Facing our most profound fears, doubts, and insecurities, we emerge victorious and transformed, able to build an enduring legacy that leaves a positive imprint on the world. Our brains crave such stories.

When you look at leaders you admire, you are likely to be drawn to their hero's journey, finding that it resonates deeply within you and inspires you to emulate or associate with them in some way. Perhaps it is a religious or spiritual figure, philosopher, community leader, philanthropist, or business leader; by becoming a follower, member, participant, employee, or customer, you make yourself part of their narrative. You are being moved, and you feel the impulse to move others in the same way, amplifying the influence of these leaders across generations and sometimes ages.

The best and most powerful stories are the ones that make us participate in them, whether or not we realize it. These narratives engage our most human of capabilities and aspirations—imagination, creativity, social connection, and the desire to transcend our current conditions and become better versions of ourselves. Stories have a magnetic effect.

Stories reinforce and amplify our existing attitudes, beliefs, and behaviors, but they can also help to change them. The stories we tell lend coherence to our everyday experience. We barely notice how much they are the result of an editorial requirement of our conscious brains. Neuroscience has given us a new appreciation for the tremendous complexity of our cognitive capacity.[9] We tend to blend facts with interpretations and associations that feel coherent and evoke the desired effect of connectedness, clarity, meaning, security, explanation, rationale, affirmation, power, purpose, or inspiration. Stories are powerful. (See Figure 4.1.)

Stories Drive Behavior

Perhaps no other industry is so centrally focused on unlocking the magnetic effect of storytelling on behavior as marketing and

> **1. Reflect on the impact specific stories and their main characters (leaders) have on you:**
> - Which stories/leaders attract, inspire, and "move" you?
> - What specifically do they inspire in you? Why?
> - How do they relate to your story or the story you would like to be able to tell?
>
> **2. What is your story OR the story you would like to tell that will inspire and "move" others?**
>
> - You may find the general structure of the hero's journey helpful. Later in this chapter, you will find a worksheet that can help you focus and create your narrative.

Figure 4.1   Putting Insights into Action

advertisement. Marketers have refined the process of discovering, developing, telling, and spreading the story of brands to attract customers and employees. Storytelling is indeed big business, considering that marketing and advertisement are global industries of roughly $44 billion and $600 billion, respectively.[10]

Lisa Lacy of Linkdex provides an insightful analysis of the stories that underpin successful brands[11] such as TOMS Shoes, Warby Parker, Chipotle, Uber, Virgin America, Airbnb, and others. She identifies seven essential elements of a successful brand story as summarized below:

1. *Start with problems.* These brands came into existence for a purpose: to address a practical problem that required a better solution or response.
2. *Embrace the underdog status.* These brands have taken on powerful and well-established competitors, disrupted the status quo, and created new ways of doing things through smarts and determination.
3. *Redefine an experience.* These brands create an experience by challenging well-established paradigms and assumptions.
4. *Foster communities of rabid fans.* These brands resonate deeply and become extensions of personal identity and lifestyle, tying together communities.

5. *Have visible founders*. These brands are personified by a charismatic, quirky, idiosyncratic, or iconic founder personality who is associated with, admired, and emulated.
6. *Know who they are and what they stand for*. These brands represent a clear sense of values and identity.
7. *Do good*. These brands aspire to add to the common good by being responsible citizens, giving back to communities and society, and helping customers and employees be their best selves.

That this list of essentials reminds us of some critical stages in the hero's journey is just another example of how deeply these elements are anchored in our shared psychological structure and the powerful effects they produce.

Many well-established organizations are learning to tell their stories more explicitly and authentically. Skanska's focus on building "for a better society,"[12] EY's on "building a better working world," and Aerotek's "our people are everything" are examples. What makes these stories powerful is that they are not empty slogans, but comprehensive and intentional efforts by their leaders to conscientiously curate a culture that actually lives its supporting value system.

We chose these three examples because of our firsthand experience with those organizations over long periods of time. They are examples of how much the motivational power of a heroic purpose (i.e., improving lives), when experienced as an actual and lived reality, supersedes a mundane purpose (i.e., selling goods or services or meeting specific revenue targets). When the latter is in service of the former, our stories become compelling. When backed up by reality, stories are irresistible and galvanize a group and community.

In other words, it is not enough to *tell* a story; you must *be* the story and engage others so that, together, you *become* the story. Or better: *the story becomes an authentic representation of the group and influences their beliefs, experiences, and behaviors.*

Leaders in these organizations have understood at a deep level that creating a narrative or storytelling works better than relaying dry presentations of charts, facts, and figures and impersonal mission and vision statements. Telling the story of what people are living and experiencing, and then engaging others in it, establishes credibility and authenticity and evokes deeper resonance and participation. Narrative is what connects us with the essential human and living core of any organization. And it is why Springsteen's quote is such a fitting statement to capture what is the essence of leading: cultivating a collective narrative that *becomes bigger than the narrative anyone could tell on their own.* Leadership could well be considered the deliberate act of *story shaping or co-creation.*

The tools of this co-creation tend to be highly dependent on two elements critical for weaving and shaping shared stories: *delivery* (how we structure the narrative and tell the story) and *leadership presence* (how we show up).

Consider the following three situations, which we have experienced firsthand in our work. As you are reading each, ask yourself how effective this approach was and how it impacted results.

At a global meeting with managers mostly from the United States, Luigi, a new leader from Italy, tried to rally his people around a new strategy. He decided to make a highly emotional pitch—he moved around the stage, and his voice and language showed his passion. His slides contained only the most essential data points, as he clearly saw his mission as being to excite his audience about the new strategy. He embellished the information on each slide with more information and detail. Slowly, Luigi built up to a deliberately crafted climax, which was a reference to a famous soccer match in which the Italian team triumphed some seven or eight years ago. He saw clear parallels between the new corporate strategy and the playing of the Italian team. The playing of the losing team also had similarities with the approach of his company's main global competitor. It was a very thoughtful metaphor. He carefully selected images from the soccer game and ordered them to correspond with his speaking points about the strategy. With great pride, Luigi also built a small video clip of the winning goal into his presentation, in which the shot was replayed three times with an ecstatic soundtrack in the background. He was sure that this would engage and excite his team, leaving a memorable emotional imprint as a shared experience for the team as they executed the strategy.

The unenthusiastic clapping at the end of his presentation immediately told Luigi that his approach did not resonate. He blamed it mostly on his audience, their limited imaginations, vision, and lack of enthusiasm. What he did not yet embrace was the idea that it was his role and responsibility as a leader to engage the audience and take them along on the journey, making them part of his story. He could have learned a lot from the informal conversations among the managers who were clustering outside the meeting room after the presentation.

They talked about how his message was unclear and that they did not understand the proposed strategy well enough. They found Luigi's effusiveness distracting, and while they got that he was passionate, they were unmoved by the soccer game imagery that seemed so meaningful to Luigi. Luigi was distracted from his central message, did not factor "them" into his presentation, and essentially used himself as the key reference point in deciding how to engage others.

It is a dangerous trap for leaders to assume that their experience is essentially a reliable guide for those they are leading, but it is especially dangerous for international professionals. The more a leader is part of the local social context, the less likely it is that this assumption is wrong, because they simply have more experiences in common. But for international professionals, it is a given that their experience is not a reliable guide to the experiences of those they lead. Luigi did not factor in that his communication style, his passion for soccer, and his emotional investment in the success of the Italian team were not simply transferrable to his audience.

After his presentation, he was deeply frustrated and concerned. He knew that his success as a leader and his internal reputation depended on successfully leading the implementation of this strategy. He worried that he had undermined his own success, putting a gap between himself and his team from which it would be difficult to recover. He was upset with himself, as he had overestimated the universal appeal of his presentation style, and he started to doubt his preparedness to lead successfully.

Anita was a high-potential employee in a U.S.-headquartered organization. She was originally from Germany and had worked for the company for six years when she was sent on a three-year assignment to Japan. Her mission was to help the local team improve the sales performance in alignment with the new global structure and processes of the organization. When she arrived in Japan she quickly saw that the team was too reactive, lacking ambition or incentives to aggressively pursue stretch goals. She decided to let some support staff go to create a leaner sales organization, change the incentive structure away from a largely team-based system to an individual performance–based system, and motivate the team members to shift their mind-set to be more proactive, optimistic, and confident in their capability to meet the aggressive corporate targets. Anita believed in swift change, and on her 10th day in Japan she gathered the team in a big meeting room and delivered what she thought was a clear, unambiguous presentation, explaining her assessment of the flailing sales performance of the team and how she had developed a specific plan to get the team "back on track." She explained the new incentive structure, processes, and expectations of each individual and the team as a whole, including a new system for tracking leads individually. She finished by giving the team a little motivational talk, stating clearly that she and her leaders in the United States had great confidence in them and were sure that these changes would help them meet their targets and significantly enhance the company's share in this important market.

Anita's presentation was only the beginning of a 15-month "nightmare," as she called it. It ended in the premature termination of her assignment and return to the United States. The changes she made demotivated the sales team, and performance further decreased rather than picking up. The team found the individual incentive program to be disruptive to their team spirit. Most important, they felt that Anita was not making herself part of the team, but that she was keeping herself at a distance. The team did not trust her to build a personal connection—and they did not believe that she was trying. In addition, they sometimes had a hard time understanding her. When she was frustrated, she spoke faster.

Anita knew things were not going well, but she was convinced that she did not have the right talent on the team. She did not feel they were a good fit with the company's values and culture, which was built on urgency, entrepreneurial spirit, and a "just get it done" attitude. She was deeply frustrated by her inability to get the team to embrace her changes and shift the way they operated. She understood why her bosses asked her to break off her assignment, but she also experienced it as a personal failure. She did not become aware of the deep disconnect, frustration, and anger her team had experienced until the team member who came to the airport to send her off said in his parting message: "Saying good-bye to you is like closing the window on a tropical storm." Needless to say, she did not have a good return flight. Only slowly did it become clear to her how deeply disconnected she was from her team and that she might have been overconfident about her leadership abilities.

Frank was from China. His Chinese name was Yingpei, but he adopted "Frank" as his English name while studying English in Tianjin. He came to the United States as a student and was delighted to be offered a position with a prestigious company in Ohio. He was driven to excel and build his career. That's why he took advantage of as many development opportunities as possible. As an engineer, he understood that his skills would take him only to a certain level and that he needed to strengthen his leadership abilities to advance. He was very active in the company's Asian Employee Resource Group, participated in most leadership training offered, and carefully observed the communication style of successful leaders. He was a diligent learner— perhaps a bit too diligent. He learned how important it was to promote himself and speak up in meetings, challenging the ideas of others. He learned that it was important to start presentations by joking and bantering, with a relaxed, casual style that also included the use of sports analogies, references to college football and baseball teams, and idiomatic expressions. Most did not see the intense effort and energy he spent in learning and adopting this recipe for success, which was reinforced through so many channels. He relentlessly prepared himself for every meeting and presentation to show up most favorably based on the cultural norms. He knew how important adapting was to success, and actively encouraged others with a similar background to follow his example and work on themselves, particularly those in the Resource Group.

Indeed, Frank built a reputation for himself. However, it was not quite the one he had intended to build. In fact, he would have been disheartened to know the impression he had on his American colleagues and those in leadership circles. He was considered to be overly pushy and aggressive, sometimes abrasive and disruptive. His casual style and joking in meetings did not seem authentic, but rather overly rehearsed and exaggerated. All this created the opposite effect of what he was hoping for: people avoided him, did not want him on their teams, and most certainly did not see him as viable leadership material. Frank sensed that his strategy did not create the desired effect, but that only fortified his resolve to work harder to adapt his workplace behavior. He was determined to crack the cultural code and break his "bamboo ceiling," as he referred to it—citing a well-known book about the cultural dilemmas of Asians, which he had taken to heart.[13] Indeed, Frank struggled with the subtle nature of the cultural code that defined the dominant norms in his organization. He was overassimilating or overcompensating—exerting excessive effort beyond what was needed in reaction to an intense feeling of inferiority, insecurity, and inadequacy.

Luigi, Anika, and Frank are but three examples of the leadership challenges faced by international professionals. They stand in for the many others who are underestimating the importance of optimizing their delivery and leadership presence in ways that use new insights into general and context-specific variables of success. Working through key aspects of delivery and presence have helped all three learn from their experience, tap it for more authentic leadership, and convert a seeming failure into the source of career success.

Delivery

How you structure your narrative and tell your story is key to "moving them." You don't want to distract your audience through verbosity, convolution, and repetition, or through metaphors that miss their desired emotional impact like Luigi's. And you do not want to be like Frank, losing your effectiveness because your inauthentic delivery makes your message unbelievable and difficult to relate to.

The following five steps are a robust and powerful guide for "moving them" regardless of whether your delivery is a single presentation or the strategic plan for your stewardship over a team, a department, or an entire organization. In the former, these five steps can help you prepare; in the latter, they can help you develop an entire leadership and communications strategy. Most leaders need a combination of both. And, as Anita's experience exemplifies, the effectiveness of your stewardship may rest on a single presentation. Or, as in Frank's case, an entire career trajectory may depend on it.

Prepare with Focus

Set time aside to *focus*, reflect, and clarify for yourself what your leadership is all about and where exactly you want them to move. This does not have to be some grandiose vision statement; rather, it is a very practical outlining of the essence of the change you want to enable (leadership is frequently connected to some kind of change). If you are not clear and focused, they will not be, either. Articulate and describe the key impact you want to make in a few clear and simple statements. Start with your objective and your "why." Most leaders underestimate the importance of communicating the "why" together with the "what" in a clear and straightforward way. The primary purpose of this is to help you stay and remain focused on the essence of your leadership.

Lars, an executive from one of the Nordic countries, wanted to integrate skilled refugees into the workforce to address current and future talent shortages in his global organization that had led to increasing demand on the existing workforce. He had realized that the refugee population was an untapped potential source for talent, and he wanted to tap it before other companies were waking up to it. While he was clear on his goal, he also knew it would not be easy. He tested his idea "softly" with some of his managers and quickly realized that he needed to contend with entrenched stereotypes, attitudes, and opinions, as well as policies and standards, if he wanted to be successful. For Lars, it was the right, moral, and socially responsible thing to do—after all, society was changing, refugees were in crisis and needed opportunities, and social isolation and marginalization of this population also posed a risk. But he was also convinced that it was the smart action to champion; after all, the company needed to build a talent pipeline of loyal and committed people. He fully recognized that this was a tall change objective, that it would not be easy, and that it would require him to stay focused for a long time. How would he engage others?

Anchor Your Message

You will need to *connect your message to "them"* in a way that helps them understand, visualize, and want the change. You need to put it into terms that are meaningful to them and compel action in a way that resonates with their experience. Personalizing is key to this goal. Just stating what you want to do factually, in an e-mail or a slide presentation, is not enough. It is neither engaging nor compelling, and you may inadvertently clutter your message with too much extraneous information, or you may dilute it by not creating the right context to make the desired impact. You will need to provide and create context to make the "what" clear and the associated actions the most natural, intuitive, and meaningful to embrace. Personalizing is an important aspect for connecting your message. You and your experience (your story) are the conduit between the content of your message (the change) and "them." You may want to reflect on questions like these: What is the connection to you and your experience? How can you create a personal connection? How does your experience connect to "them" or reflect on their experience?

> Lars thought long and hard about how he could best personalize his focus, engage others, and move them and the organization along. Personalizing required him to model the behavior he asked others to engage in. He decided to mentor refugees who had the basic skills he was looking for. He engaged with aid organizations to identify such individuals, and selected two he felt confident about. He scheduled his mentoring meetings in the office, so that others could see and become curious. He also learned a lot about the needs and situations of refugees, and engaged with human resources and other functions to fund a sort of internship program for the refugees. He learned that the pathway to opening opportunities was by inspiring social connections through which biases and stereotypes could be reduced and potential value created.

Deepen Their Interest

Now, you can *tell the story* and develop the shared narrative. When you do that, the discussion on storytelling and narrative earlier in this chapter holds some great advice. You need to first deepen their interest and grab their attention. This is more than just telling or recounting your story, but finding a way to engage their emotions, experience, curiosity, and imaginations. Most important, it needs to be true and not made up for the effect.

> Lars traced his focus back to an initial spark that made him realize that he should do something to help refugee populations. He was sitting at the dinner table with his son, after both had watched a documentary on the refugee crisis that discussed the risks and opportunities associated with the integration of refugees. His son asked Lars a simple question: "And what are you doing about this?" Lars was both struck and embarrassed. "Here was an obvious situation right under my nose and I was not doing anything!" He felt ashamed that he did not have a good answer for his son, and he wanted to be a good role model of taking social responsibility. Many leaders might leave this initial spark out of their story—it may seem too personal or not relevant—but it is often powerful. Who cannot relate to the discomfort of acting counter to one's values, or the feeling of embarrassment when those to whom you want to be a role model are challenging you? It is hard to argue with Lars's experience, and it invites a personal query about one's own values and their alignment with one's action. As an explanation for why Lars then reached out and mentored refugees, it created a cohesive and inspiring story. That Lars modeled the behavior invited others to follow suit. But he did not ask them to do the same. He simply let his story linger for a while.

Hold Their Attention

It is important to *hold their attention* and keep them mentally and emotionally engaged. The elements that are central to this are conflict, vividness, and detail. Conflict creates curiosity: What's next? How will the story continue? Vividness is key to *drawing others in* and *making them part of the story*—vividness means providing sensory information, and it becomes the proxy for real experience. It makes us feel as though we were directly involved and part of the experience.

> When Lars talked about his embarrassment when his son asked this challenging question, the audience became drawn in. By not simply listing actions he would like his audience to engage in and letting people sit with their own introspection, he was holding their attention. He also told his audience what he learned and what the refugees gained from his mentoring relationship. Besides appreciating the difficult situation, he learned about the skills and background they possessed that could be productively utilized. He also developed a specific idea of what kind of support they needed. He talked about his experience as a "gift."

Articulate What Makes the Positive Difference

Clearly identifying and articulating what makes a positive difference is the critical ingredient of transformation. The positive difference is key to inspiring others to follow suit and apply a new skill and technique. Use a simple, compelling, and memorable metaphor or event through which the change becomes attainable and real. This helps your audience visualize clearly the actions to take.

> Lars, building on the idea of the "gift," now did something else. A holiday was coming up, and he arranged for everyone to receive a gift from him. The gift was a mentoring relationship paired with the invitation to learn together and evaluate how this dormant talent pool could best be tapped. First building credibility by personally engaging in this behavior and then holding his audience's attention

on his message over a period of time were key to his gifts being appreciated and accepted with curiosity and anticipation. He rallied a diverse group of leaders and is proud of the results: a thriving mentoring and apprenticeship program for qualified refugees, a deepened relationship with the public sector, which also translated into commercial value, and—critically—a sense of pride, purpose, and community among the key leaders in his business unit.

Lars is an inspiring example of practicing leadership in a diverse, global organization that did not depend on superb command of the English language—in fact, he did not feel very confident about his English skills and had a bit of an inferiority complex toward native speakers, particularly when he observed them present with ease, poise, and charisma. Lars also did not need incredible presentation skills—he was not a charismatic presenter in that way at all. In the end, he needed none of these to move others.

Lars's example is instructive and can challenge us to look beyond our narrow English skills or presentation abilities to other attributes that enable us to tell a compelling, moving story. It does not have to be at the level and scale of Lars's example, either. The simple lesson to draw from this example and discussion is that delivery (i.e., storytelling) is not a technique composed of presentation tips and tricks, but an embrace of us, in our three-dimensional experience, as the story. We just need to share it in all its dimensions.

While Lars was very deliberate, we may only slowly discover the stories within us that end up inspiring and compelling action we did not preconceive. Sometimes we become aware of them almost by accident or through external prompting. During a recent panel discussion designed to explore common career challenges and how to navigate them, two panelists stumbled into a new understanding of their relationship with English, much to their own surprise. They had suppressed their feelings for decades, but a few simple, pointed questions elicited an expression of authentic experience that resonated with the sizable number of non-native speakers in the audience, who were inspired and found role models for an experience that they rarely talked about and in which they had felt rather alone.

Alejandro, one of the panelists, was born in Colombia. When he was nine years old, his family moved to a rural part of the United States. He had a difficult time learning English and was bullied and teased about his accent and his English language skills. He grew very sensitive and tried his best to sound as close to native as possible, but retained a rather strong Spanish accent. His family moved back to Colombia after four years, where he finished high school. For several reasons, he went to study in the United States and found a job at a professional services company. One of his managers made a decision to pair him with a native English speaker for an important presentation because the manager told Alejandro that his "accent was still too strong" and he did not want to "risk making the wrong impression." For the first time, Alejandro found himself talking about how this comment triggered a tremendous insecurity in him. This was a pivotal experience, as it strengthened his resolve to embrace and be proud of his accent and make it the characteristic of his professional brand—just like we discussed and recommend in Chapter 2. He talked about it as "finding the courage to be confident about who you are." Alejandro became quite emotional about his experience, and the audience was riveted by his willingness to be real and vulnerable about his inner turmoil.

This triggered the second panelist, Gloria, to speak about her experience with language. She spoke with a clear U.S. accent, and most would have easily placed her background in the Midwest of the United States. That she was born and raised in Jamaica, West Indies, came as a big surprise to many in the audience. She then spoke about the intense, self-imposed rigor she had lived by—ever since she had harbored the dream to emigrate to the United

States—to assimilate into the mainstream by training the Jamaican accent out of her speech and relentlessly rehearsing to sound like "an American." Aided by a VHS video recorder, she would replay and imitate U.S. newscasts, often for hours. Later, when her dream had come true and she had moved to the United States, she built an amazing career taking on more hurdles associated with race (she was Black) and gender in a traditionally white and male industry. By straightening her hair, always being extra prepared, and learning how to lead like the men around her, she excelled in her career. But to do this she had to sacrifice her identity, of which she was rightfully proud, to remake it in the image of her surroundings. Something in Alejandro's story, most likely his emotion, resonated with her, and the magnitude of the constraints she was placing on herself became apparent. She did not find the courage of her own confidence, but built up her own confidence by molding herself in the image of success she found around her.

These are examples of the powerful connection we can unlock by becoming aware of the stories embedded in our experience. To connect better and more deeply, we may need to develop the courage to find the story in our own life and experience. We may indeed be the story that moves them. (See Figure 4.2.)

Leadership Presence

All of us have presence. It is our way of showing up in a group and the energy that we bring to it. In the context of leadership, however, the term *presence* is often used to refer to the effect that some people evoke because they seem to naturally attract attention and pull the focus of others toward them, seemingly without effort. *Presence* is an important factor for being perceived as a leader. As an international professional, it may be critical for you to understand and appraise your

The lessons learned about storytelling can, of course, be applied to improve your leadership communication on a more basic level—the way you present. Here are a few things you can do to apply these principles:

Observe and analyze presentations that grab your attention and capture you. The most popular TED talks for example also tend to be good examples of the five elements we discussed:

1. Focus
2. Anchor your message
3. Deepen interest
4. Hold attention
5. Articulate what makes the positive difference

Watch these talks repeatedly and identify these elements.

Apply these elements to the next time you give a presentation that encourages others to embrace a change, deepen their understanding, or take action. Make sure you are not applying a formula but tap your own authenticity in the process. Seek out specific feedback to learn about your effectiveness.

Figure 4.2   Lessons Learned about Storytelling

presence in the context of the *predominant presence expectations* in your environment.

After all, leadership effectiveness tends to be highly contextual—that is, dependent on the societal and organizational norms, beliefs, and values that are enshrined and reinforced in the stories and hero myths of these environments. Developing contextual or situational awareness is a key success factor for you as an international professional, together with the behavioral skill to shift style appropriately and authentically based on that context or situation. As we will see, this requires a delicate balance between being grounded in an authentic sense of self and using a flexible behavioral repertoire to communicate your intended message.

The GLOBE Study[14] is an ambitious and comprehensive empirical project that can help us decipher the various codes of leadership presence from an international perspective. A macro-level study to illuminate leadership from a cross-cultural perspective, the GLOBE

Study discerns clusters of value orientations that constitute six normative leadership styles and their relative geographic predominance.
Accordingly, the GLOBE Study recognizes:

> **Performance-oriented leadership** (*also referred to as "charismatic/
> value-based"*)   This style stresses high standards, decisiveness, and
> innovation; seeks to inspire people around a vision; creates a passion
> among them to perform; and does so by firmly holding on to core
> values.
>
> **Team-oriented leadership**   This style instills pride, loyalty, and
> collaboration among organizational members, and highly values team
> cohesiveness and a common purpose or goal.
>
> **Participative leadership**   This style encourages input from others
> in decision making and implementation, and emphasizes delegation
> and equality.
>
> **Humane leadership**   This style stresses compassion and generosity,
> and it is a patient, supportive, and other-centered approach.
>
> **Autonomous leadership**   This style emphasizes an independent,
> individualistic, and self-centered approach.
>
> **Self-protective leadership**   This style emphasizes procedure, status
> consciousness, and face saving, focused on the safety and security of the
> individual and/or the group.

As with most cross-cultural analyses of this kind, these typologies
are not pure in their expression, nor can we simply associate them with
specific geographies. However, the study suggests specific combina-
tions of leadership styles as normative for specific cultural clusters, such
as Anglo, Nordic, Germanic, Confucian, Middle Eastern, African, and
others. While these are no doubt broad generalizations, we find them
preferable to simplistic national profiles (after all, national boundaries
are political, not cultural, boundaries). But as with any cross-cultural
analyses, we cannot consider them as predictive of specific individuals
or circumstances.

They are most useful when we consider them as validation of the reality of cultural differences and a broad-stroking orientation to the nature of differences and similarities, which help us understand the lived experience in intercultural relationships. If we understand them as general patterns, validated in one of the most ambitious and comprehensive research efforts, they become useful for reflecting upon our experiences and can help us understand the experiences of international professionals from a broader context. This understanding needs to be translated into specific navigational strategies, as we will see.

The study, for example, indicates that the Middle Eastern cluster (which includes Turkey, Egypt, or Morocco), with a normative preference for a self-protective leadership style and low levels of participative and performance-oriented styles, shows up as most distinct from the Anglo cluster (which includes England, the United States, Australia, and Canada, among others), with a normative preference for performance-oriented and participative styles. The Germanic cluster of Germany, the Netherlands, Austria, and Switzerland, with its blend of performance-oriented, participative, and autonomous styles, shows up as most distinct from the Confucian cluster of China, South Korea, and Japan, which tends to prefer self-protective, humane, and team-oriented styles, and lesser resonance with a participative style.

These are just some examples of the general tendencies the study enables. They alert international professionals and the organizations they work for to the hidden risks posed by different normative style preferences, the likelihood of derailment, and the specific gaps to close to become fully effective and gain traction in their careers and lives abroad.

These insights put into perspective Anita's failure in Japan that we discussed earlier. She built the narrative that she wanted the Japanese sales team to embrace a value and belief system that did not resonate with them. Her narrative reflected the autonomous and performance-oriented style that became part of her professional presence due to the social conditioning embedded in her personal and professional biography. Unfortunately, this clashed with the team-oriented, self-protective, and humane expectation held by many of the Japanese she was working with. Anita established her presence based on assumptions that seemed natural and normal for her, and she neither fathomed nor prepared for the likelihood that they would not work in her new context. Anything but clinical, these gaps express themselves through difficult and emotional experiences, full of frustration, anger, and doubt.

What Anita needed most was what she was least prepared for. We call it style shifting. This is the ability to show up differently to communicate your intended message and have the desired impact (i.e., "move them"). Style shifting works with the natural plasticity of human behavior but extends it purposefully to situations where the behavioral code is predictably different from the ones we are used to or expect based on our cultural conditioning. Even when English is the common mode for communication, if the underlying expectations of our counterparts are anchored in a significantly different worldview and cultural orientation, we will fail to communicate, connect, and be effective. In other words, even if our words are understood, our intentions may not be, and therefore our message may not translate. This has been the experience not only of Luigi, Anita, and Frank, but also of many who are leading in English.

Style Shifting

Style shifting is the ability to use a broad behavioral repertoire in a context- or situation-specific way to communicate your intended message and achieve your desired objective.

Style shifting is the deliberate and temporary use of a different behavioral approach (style) because you understand that in a different context, where different norms and expectations prevail, a different style will result in a better outcome.

Most of us understand the fundamental idea easily when it comes to very overt norms, such as customs, etiquette, and protocol. Most people who are not used to eating with chopsticks, with their hands, or with fork and knife gladly learn to when traveling and spending time among people who do. Who would not learn to hand over a business card with both hands and oriented it so your recipient can read it when you know this is the norm? However, style shifting becomes harder to do when it comes to situations in which we have deeply held beliefs and expectations around how we and others should behave.

One of the most common arenas in which styles clash is in meetings. Let's assume you are a team-oriented leader—in the language of the GLOBE research—and you have an hour-long meeting scheduled with a new colleague. Your natural or more authentic style might be to spend most of that time getting to know your colleague, and relatively little time might be spent talking about the job to be done or the task at hand. If your style is reflective of the dominant norm and the expectation of the new colleague, you will have a good meeting. However, if your styles are mismatched, your counterpart may wonder about you and your effectiveness and may find you odd, and the relationship may not start on the right footing. You may need to observe your counterpart carefully and shift your style, or you may want to set expectations right up front so that you first negotiate the expectations of your first meeting. Both strategies work better than simply assuming your expectations and natural style are a reliable guide to approach this situation.

As an international professional, you are more likely to need style-shifting skills, as by definition you operate in and across contexts and environments in which you are not native. In our experience, too many of you have spent little time exploring your experiences and challenging yourselves on the effectiveness of your style. There is a tendency to minimize the importance of style shifting when it comes to presence, as the examples of Luigi, Anita, and Frank clearly illustrate. We may perceive our style to work well because we *feel* successful, but we may not be aware of the disconnect that suboptimizes our effectiveness, and we may have never seriously explored whether we could enhance our effectiveness significantly. Or we feel that we cannot connect, and we blame this problem on other aspects, rather than on our own intercultural adaptation. In the case of a significant clash, we may also blame it on the other or on unfavorable circumstances.

Martin, an international from Germany, described the deep personal challenge he experienced when trying to enhance his ability to connect better and communicate with native English-speaking counterparts, both British and U.S. American. He needed to make frequent sales presentations and build rapport. He felt that his authentic approach was at odds with the patterns that seemed to work for others, especially when it came to small talk and the customary joking and banter that was an important part of succeeding. He received feedback that he needed to be less formal and to "lighten up"—not be so serious—and try to make his audiences laugh, as this would engage them and make them feel at ease.

But he struggled, not because he could not laugh or be informal. Rather, he felt that making sales presentations to relative strangers in this style seemed inappropriate and inauthentic. He was doubtful that prospective customers would respond well to what seemed overtly manipulative and not neutral enough for the potential customer to feel empowered. But he also recognized that he was in a different environment, where a different style would be more effective.

Martin realized that he needed to adopt a different style, as he could see the success of this pattern in his peers. He had to learn to associate a new style with situations in which it seemed unfitting; in other words, he needed to shift his experience and the feelings that inhibited him to show up differently.

Martin wholeheartedly embraced this challenge and sought out a peer mentor whom he would observe intently and who would observe him and provide feedback. He also structured situations for himself in which he could practice this style, to improve his own comfort zone. It felt like role playing at first—not natural or authentic—and he was quite stressed and self-conscious. With increasing practice, his comfort levels increased, particularly as he could feel that his audiences were also becoming more responsive and the positive resonance of their reaction encouraged him to continue. The increasing comfort eventually brought about a sense of authenticity, and he could integrate this style into his repertoire so that it was now available in situations where that style was better suited to express his intention. Now when Martin needed to engage his audience and make them positively disposed toward the services of his company, he could make the shift.

Developing the ability to style shift is not an easy undertaking, as it involves challenging deep-seated assumptions and associations, and managing the emotions that arise when we do so. It leads to an expansion of one's comfort zone to embrace a behavior that we might otherwise not choose. Importantly, it relies on developing situational awareness and asking ourselves whether we are more attached to a specific behavior or to communicating our intended message in a context-appropriate way.

When considering style shifting as a strategy to build a more expansive leadership presence across context and situations, authenticity becomes essential. There is a tendency to see authenticity as an individual attribute. However, we can also see it as a quality of a relationship, involving the complex interactions of intentions, motivations, attitudes, behaviors, and sentiments that characterize the communication between two or more people. Authenticity, perceived in this manner, is preserved when we choose a behavior that communicates our intention in a way that is clearly understood by the other (not always in the way that we prefer). A simple example can illustrate this point. To communicate my respect for someone, I may avoid eye contact in certain circumstances. Even though it may be an unfamiliar and uncommon expression of my true intention, it allows me to stay true to the essence of my sentiment.

The effective use of style shifting is therefore critically enabled by a highly developed level of empathy and social resonance. Leaders need to be attuned to the emotional undercurrent of their interactions, accurately repairing and preventing social dissonance. Empathy and social resonance guarantee the authenticity that makes style shifting a credible aspect of leadership presence in the first place. It is worthwhile to emphasize that style shifting is very different from assimilation. Style shifting is a deliberate strategy that is a temporary and situation-dependent way to get the intended message across effectively. Assimilation is a form of permanent suppression or masking of aspects of oneself as a success strategy to avoid negative repercussions, prejudicial attitudes, and biases.

The line between style shifting and assimilation may seem blurry, but it is profound. Gloria, the panelist we encountered earlier, chose an assimilation strategy. Assimilation can lead to career success, but it is associated with a personal cost. Ultimately, assimilation is based on limiting and censoring oneself, whereas style shifting is about an expansion of a repertoire, akin to acquiring another language or two to expand your communicative reach. Style shifting ultimately enables individuals to preserve their original style and build upon it, rather than abandoning or suppressing it as with assimilation. The distinction is critical, for the former enables one to confidently flourish and leads to inner groundedness, whereas the latter is accompanied by a conflict of identity. However, we recognize that this distinction, in reality, can be unclear. International professionals frequently struggle with this. A Ghanaian woman, after four years working in the United States, explains the acute dilemma she feels in the following way:

> There is an expectation to "speak up," to toot your own horn, and to focus on advancing yourself. This conflicts with what I learned growing up about reverence for authority, respect, and the belief that hard work will be recognized and rewarded. It seems that you should be very political and have ulterior motives when you build relationships in the U.S. That does not seem authentic.

She articulates the pressure many experience when leading in English. And she will need to navigate a narrow path between assimilation and style shifting to enhance her career. We are convinced that building style-shifting skills addresses the most fundamental causes of distance and disconnect so frequently reported by international professionals. Most important, it is the positive resolution of a pervasive inner conflict that international professionals face—whether or not they do so consciously.

This inner conflict is aggravated by messages and models of leadership presence that try to ignore or even deny the culturally contingent nature of the concept to begin with. A study of executive presence conducted by the Center for Talent Innovation (CTI) provides relevant insights for the U.S.-dominated context, but may have less value from an international perspective.[15] In fact, it can serve as an instructive example of a culturally contingent notion of leadership and executive presence that impacts so many seeking to build careers in organizations where U.S. values are the predominant cultural influence of leadership standards.

According to CTI, executive presence accounts for 26 percent of what it takes to get promoted. The study deconstructs this elusive concept into gravitas, communication, and appearance, but not with equal importance or proportion. Gravitas shows up as the most important factor. The study breaks it down as a composite impression based on six components: confidence and "grace under fire," decisiveness and "showing teeth," integrity (defined as "speaking truth to power"), emotional intelligence, reputation and standing, and vision or charisma.

Communication is somewhat less important, and comprises superior speaking skills, ability to command a room, assertiveness, ability to read the audience, sense of humor, ability to banter, body language, and posture. *Appearance* is the least important of the factors, with grooming and polish, physical attractiveness, and sophisticated clothing scoring relatively highly within this factor.

Our conjecture is that these findings reveal the predominant performance-oriented leadership style (in the language of GLOBE research), that is, an ethnocentric and male-templated version of presence that international professionals contend with. This interpretation is supported when considering that women and ethnic minorities reported struggling more with executive presence. Of minority professionals, 56 percent indicated that they felt held to a higher standard, whereas 31 percent of the white majority believe non-Caucasians are held to a stricter code. Also, 81 percent of women in the study who received feedback indicated that feedback on executive presence was contradictory, and they were left confused about how to act on it.

We would advise you to examine your experience of this dominant style expectation in your environment and evaluate the degree to which your leadership presence effectiveness and career growth are stifled or undermined. This includes identifying situations where a sense of discomfort and inner tension undermines your effectiveness. Finally, evaluate how style shifting could be a viable resolution strategy to help expand your leadership effectiveness.

Organizations may also want to engage with their population of international professionals to better understand their experiences and identify the barriers and challenges they experience within the corporate culture. That includes evaluating the embedded implicit cultural biases, making them explicit, seeking to reduce them, and assisting international professionals in style-shifting skills. This is even more critical for organizations seeking to strengthen their global leadership pipelines in response to the acutely felt global talent shortage.[16]

Implications for International Professionals

What are the specific lessons that you may want to draw from this chapter? What should you take to heart?

- As an international professional, you are not unique in your journey to develop and grow your leadership capability. It is helpful to understand and internalize the power of storytelling and narrative as a critical element for connecting with and moving others.
- Leadership, understood as the capability "to move them," obtains added dimensions as international professionals are invariably more foreign and therefore removed from the people they seek to move. You are well advised to build added skills in relation to your delivery and leadership presence in a context- and situation-aware manner.
- To refine and optimize your delivery, you are well advised not to focus on technique first, but on discovering your story first. The personal experience with foreignness can and should become a critical part of that story.
- Applying our five-step framework can help you effectively tell stories, whether preparing for a single speech or presentation or planning the course of your stewardship over a team, a department, or an entire organization.
- Leadership presence is highly culturally dependent, and international professionals frequently struggle with finding their way between the prevalent norms and expectations of their environment and their own sense of authenticity. Style shifting is a consciously honed skill that can help you find a comfortable balance.

International professionals in leadership roles have to contend with the formidable challenge of "moving them" (i.e., converge and transform the motivations, perceptions, and behaviors of individuals and groups). This is not easy in any language or cultural context. However, the disadvantage of international professionals actually may turn out to be an advantage. As we have seen through many representative examples, they navigate the challenges of effective, deliberate communication in English and with different audiences and in various contexts. They challenge themselves and their abilities at very personal levels. They learn strategies on how to connect and build rapport with native speakers. Most importantly, they recover, build, and increase their confidence in unfamiliar environments—hopefully, in organizations that understand and support the challenges these leaders face daily.

To harness this advantage, native and non-native English speakers, and the organizations they serve, need to pay deliberate attention and cultivate awareness, understanding, and engage carefully calibrated support.

Back at the Lounge

"Excuse me?"

Pierre heard a pleasant voice behind him, and as he was turning around he exclaimed to the group, "Finally! That must be my am-buh—"

But it was not his hamburger. Instead he saw a stylish, sophisticated woman with a playful smile in her dark eyes.

Pierre quickly recovered. "I am so very sorry. Please excuse my error," he apologized as a faint flush ran up his cheeks.

Liz jumped in. "He really has been waiting quite some time!"

Still smiling, the woman graciously nodded, and said, "It's absolutely okay! I have to say—I couldn't help but overhear your conversation. Do you mind if I join you?" They voiced their assent all at once, so she pulled up a chair. A larger table had opened in the lounge 15 minutes ago, and the group had moved there to continue their conversation more comfortably.

"What is your name?" asked Wendy.

"I'm Sofia—and yours?" As she looked at each of them, they went around the table introducing themselves. "Well, it's a pleasure to meet you."

Her presence had a magical impact on the group. They sensed she had been to many places and experienced all the wonders and challenges they had been talking about. She quietly and eloquently

135

revealed her background. Sofia was an Argentine native who had lived in many countries, transcended linguistic and cultural differences, and shattered the glass ceiling to become a senior executive at a large multinational in Seoul.

"That's amazing," said Toshi, his eyes full of admiration. But they soon clouded, as a thought came into his head. "Please forgive me, but it can't have been an easy journey."

"You're right, Toshi, it wasn't easy, and I made a lot of mistakes along the way. My faux pas became the stepping-stones for a successful career. Most people do not realize that inside the mistakes are wonderfully packaged messages that reveal to us the paths we must take. In fact, that was what I was here in LA to talk about."

"How so?" asked Liz.

"I was invited to speak at a cross-cultural leadership conference about my experience as a global leader. As I told the audience, 'my journey was filled with turbulence, determination, and connection.'"

"Why do I always get sent to boring conferences when I could be learning about something that mattered to me?" said Pierre, indignantly and with good humor. Everyone laughed.

"It really was quite wonderful. I wish that I had been able to attend such a conference before I started my career—I would've avoided a lot of heartache!" Sofia sighed wistfully. "I'm quite a private person and I normally keep to myself when I travel, but when I heard you talking about the challenges you were facing as international professionals I knew that I would feel terrible if I didn't share with you some of the things that I learned."

"Yes, please tell us!" Wendy surprised everyone with the enthusiasm in her voice.

"I'd be glad to. I wish I could tell you that it's all about celebrating differences, kindness, and compassion. . . ."

"For sure, but what else?" asked Wendy.

"All right, perhaps I can share with you some of the unconventional wisdom that I have uncovered over the years working and leading in English. First, have any of you ever danced before?" asked Sofia, with a twinkle in her eye.

"Well, yes, of course; put on some good music and no one can help but dance, at least a little," pointed out Pierre. He was enjoying this conversation.

"Okay, let me rephrase that," said Sofia. "Have any of you ever taken dance lessons?"

"I did ballet when I was a little girl," remembered Liz. "But that was a lo-o-o-ong time ago."

"So, Sofia, you dance, then?" inquired Wendy.

"Yes!" Sofia's face lit up. "I have always loved to dance. And my favorite dance is the tango—it's in my blood! You should try it sometime—I think you would like it. But my point isn't to sign you up for tango lessons. We can learn a lot about communicating in English by looking at the similarities with tango. In both cases, it's crucial for both partners to try to pay close attention to each other. Imagine a dance in which one partner is not even trying—it will never work! The connection between the two partners is the heart and soul of any harmony they hope to achieve. If they are not synchronized, they will only end up frustrating each other."

"And stepping on each other's toes," interjected Toshi, with a knowing smile.

"Exactly," said Sofia. "In the same way, both native and non-native English speakers need to try to understand one another. There's a great idiom in English—'it takes two to tango.' A lot of the time we are so focused on what we need to change in ourselves, especially when it comes to our accents, that we forget that there is another person involved. It is a two-way street.

"Wisdom number one: speak clearly—it's about you. Focus on the clarity of your communication, not on your accent."

Sofia added, "My friends, your accent is actually your competitive advantage. It has been mine! We're obsessed with reducing our accent to the point that we end up focusing more on the form than on what we're trying to communicate. No wonder we're often exhausted after work."

Pierre had an aha! moment. "So focusing on my accent is a trap! My accent is my brand. I'd better start capitalizing on it."

Sofia smiled and told the group: "Now that you have spotted the trap, always remember two things: the clarity of your communication is the name of the game! And it takes two to tango. Native speakers need to learn to be comfortable with different accents. I have learned at this conference that non-native accented English is the new norm in organizations around the world. Non-native speakers are now the majority in many organizations.

"Wisdom number two: speak with impact—it's about them." Sofia ordered a soda and added: "Once you've started the tango, you've got to keep it going!

"Confidence and clarity are intricately connected and mutually dependent. Once you've done the work internally to improve your mind-set, confidence, and clarity of speech, it's time to stop thinking about yourself and start thinking about the impact you are having on your audience.

"Look, my secret is to RAP." The group looked at her strangely. "Yes, I have learned to RAP: Recognize. Affirm. Participate. I even taught it to the senior managers who report to me in Seoul. I also used this formula to help me give my speech at the conference."

Wendy asked Sofia: "How does this work?"

Sophia answered, "Let me use the conference as an example. There were close to 300 people at my keynote." Pierre leaned in a bit closer to listen.

"First, I recognized my audience by pointing out a few friends I had seen there, mentioned the multiple industries present, and then, most important, acknowledged the entire audience as fellow international professionals who all share similar turbulence and triumphs. The purpose is to recognize that we all belong to this same community.

"Then, I affirmed why they should be listening. I actually put this into a value proposition statement that said: 'Your success and your organization's success depend on your ability to dance the tango—to get along with one another and collaborate regardless of the languages you speak or the country in which you were born.'

"Finally, I asked them to participate, and taught them a new skill: to listen and link. I asked them to share stories with one another and link their experiences together.

"Their interactions during my talk allowed all of us to share in the collective wisdom in the room. Our stories together are powerful and convincing.

"Wisdom number three: Develop a compelling narrative—it's about moving them.

"Let me share with you some interesting leadership attributes that do not get enough attention," said Sofia. "It's using storytelling and style shifting."

Sofia then asked the lounge participants to take a moment to share a success story, and challenged them to link these stories into their own experiences. The group loved the exercise and learned more about one another. They enjoyed linking their stories together to create a memorable experience that they would carry forward.

"I use storytelling in almost all my speeches and meetings to inspire others. Everyone needs to be always authentic, but they also need to do homework about the people who are listening to them.

"Developing a compelling narrative is not about one story that best describes who you are, but rather multiple stories, examples, and scenarios that create a narrative about who you are and what you represent. It becomes your brand that answers the questions: What drives you? What values do you have that are non-negotiable? The 'compelling' part of the story is perhaps most important. You must connect with your audiences so that they too can resonate with your story. That is how you move them. This leadership characteristic does not get enough attention in traditional training programs and learning engagements. To reach that inner space that motivates people, we need to be flexible—not in our message, but in our delivery of it."

Sofia asked the group to reflect on the stories that they had just shared with one another and how they might have shifted their style based on who they were speaking with.

Liz thought that she had to slow down her speech just a bit when communicating with Pierre, but she also used her normal vocabulary.

Pierre, on the other hand, was now fascinated by the idea of using his accent as a brand and knew that Liz, with her international experience, would be able to understand him well. He also used a little more emphasis in key spots to ensure she got the message.

"Style shifting," Sophia went on to explain, "is a very powerful tool to temporarily change your preferred style of communication so that you can deliver messages accurately in different contexts and cultures.

"We, as international professionals, need to be good at style shifting because we are working across various languages and cultures, and we want others to understand our core message."

Liz, thinking of her experience in Brazil, said to Sofia, "This is easier said than done! I really need to get better at it."

Sophia smiled again and added, "I know it takes practice."

Sofia's phone buzzed. She looked down and sighed. "Unfortunately, it looks like it's time for me to head out."

They were all sad to see her go, and thanked her for her wisdom and for sharing her experience.

"I'll ask about your hamburger on the way out," said Sofia, winking at Pierre. Pierre smiled and ruefully shook his head.

At the same time, they all heard the message through the lounge's loudspeaker: "All planes are now ready for boarding!"

Now it was time to go to their gates. As they said good-bye and exchanged business cards, something remarkable, spontaneous, and genuine happened. They all embraced and wished one another the best of luck.

As they did so, they saw the bartender standing directly behind them. Liz realized that he had listened to part of their conversation with Sofia. He smiled at Liz as if to say, "Hey, I learned something, too."

On their way to their gates, everybody was thinking about all their discussions, the valuable time with Sofia, and what they would do next.

Liz will try to empathize more with her Brazilian colleagues, who might be intimidated about speaking in English with her. She will be careful using idioms and explain them when she does. She will think about a story she can use that will motivate her team, knowing that she will need to understand their world first.

Toshi is determined that he will stop trying to be perfect. He is going to adopt some of the recovery strategies. He will work on developing his ability to style shift to contribute in meetings, realizing that it does not mean he is being rude or arrogant in that context.

Wendy is going to stop worrying about her accent and will work on vocal variety and communicating with passion and enthusiasm. Ultimately, she will try to focus more on her audience, rather than herself. She will own her accent as a unique part of her story.

Pierre will use work-arounds and not do the same thing repeatedly when he's not being understood, like with the bartender. He also will talk to the executive team of his company about how they can raise awareness and create an inclusive environment for international professionals, native and non-native. It's long overdue that the playing field be level and equal.

As Pierre's flight took off, he reflected on the discussions at the lounge. As the plane reached 10,000 feet, his stomach began to growl. Luckily the flight attendant had just started to take everyone's order for the in-flight meal. Pierre pulled out the menu and scanned the choices. Perfect.

The flight attendant reached Pierre's seat, asking, "And what can I get for you?"

"I would like to order the am–buh–gah," Pierre replied, pointing on the menu.

"Of course, sir."

As the flight attendant began to turn around, Pierre's stomach growled even louder and a look of panic crossed his face. "Please wait!" He had decided not to test fate twice in the same day. "I've changed my mind. I will go with the fish."

Toolkit

Four-Step Process for Clear Speaking

Assess It!

If you are self-conscious about your accent or suspect that your accent hinders your relationships and opportunities, and are considering accent modification, a professional assessment may be helpful. However, you may need to adjust your end goal. The objective should not be to sound as close to native speech as possible. Rather, you should strive to reduce any aspects of your accent and/or speech pattern that seriously impede being understood. Besides being easier to achieve, it is the only reason that would ever warrant any accent modification work. If you decide on a professional assessment, be aware that most providers do not share this perspective. Many have an incentive to turn you into a client and may want to sell you long and expensive programs.

Embrace It!

Most non-native and native speakers who are self-conscious about their accent should adopt Henry Kissinger as their role model and self-confidently embrace their accent as their distinctive trademark. We cannot overemphasize the importance of this. Turning self-consciousness into confidence is not an easy transformation at all. It takes deliberate attention and a diligent personal program.

Name It!

Address your sensitivity and others' perception bias head-on! When presenting yourself, acknowledge your sensitivity and call out prevalent biases. You may say something like: "I know I have an accent, and you may think I am not as effective in pitching business. But I am very convincing, as my track record shows." Or, you may say, "You may think that because my accent means I did not grow up here that I do not know how to relate to our stakeholders. However, in my work history, I have always built strong relationships with people who were different from me." Sometimes it is enough to just name your self-consciousness, such as "I know I have a strong accent, and I hope it does not get in your way to hear my message."

Leverage It!

As Paula and Kasia's team experience illustrates, the very act of paying deliberate attention to sharing the experience with language and communication in English can be an important trigger that inspires attitudes and habits within a team that are integral to overall performance as a team. Listening better, communicating more deliberately, helping and supporting one another—all these can be critical byproducts of sharing vulnerabilities connected to language, cultivating norms that help everyone, and easing the subtle and not so subtle stress induced by a dominant English language norm.

Difficult Sound Exercises

Work-Arounds

Force your audience to understand you by indicating the context in which you are using the word.

Classic work-arounds when sounds fail:

1. *Sound "Th":* when "three" sounds like "tree"; when "thirty" sounds like "dirty"

   Example   "We have 'dirty' bullet points."

   Work-Around   "We have 'dirty'—as in the number—bullet points." Let people know you are indicating the number 30.

2. *Sounds "L" and "R":* when you cannot distinguish between "word" and "world"

   Example   "It is big 'word.'"

   Work-Around   "It is a big 'word' that we live in." By adding a short phrase, you will help everyone understand that you are referring to the planet.

3. *Sounds "L" and "R":* when a difficult word like "growl" sounds like "gwowa"

   Example   "I heard a 'gwowa.'"

   Work-Around   "I heard a dog 'gwowa' or an animal 'gwowa.'" Provide context so that "growl" can be understood.

The word "growl" is one of the most difficult words in the English language to use for many speakers of Asian languages. That is why we included it here. You can simply avoid using this word. You can use a work-around by saying simply, "The dog made a deep and menacing sound."

4. *Sounds "V" and "W"*: when you cannot distinguish between "Vic" and "Wick" or when "water" sounds like "vater"

   Example   "'Wick' was here."

   Work-Around   "'Wick,' my friend, was here." Provide context to force understanding.

   Example   "The 'vater' is cold."

   Work-Around   "The drinking 'vater' is cold." Again, context forces the audience to understand the difficult sound.

5. *Sounds "V" and "B"*: when you cannot distinguish between "vote" and "boat"

   Example   "The 'vote' is in."

   Work-Around   "The 'vote' for the election is in."

Exercise for Versatility of Expression

Take the overused expression and generate five different ways to say the same thing. An example is provided for you. Purpose: become more versatile when you cannot find the right word.

COMMON EXPRESSIONS	TRUE MEANING	EXAMPLE OF EXPRESSING YOUR IDEA
At the end of the day	When all has been considered	Regardless, we all must still perform the tests
Par for the course	The norm	The project is on course
It is what it is	The actual state	We can't change that...we should accept the situation
It's not rocket science	Not a high degree of difficulty	We should be able to easily figure this out...
Let me circle back to you	Follow up	I'll reach out when I have more info
At this moment in time	Now, but the situation may change	Right now we can accomplish...

The Accent Cycle in Organizations

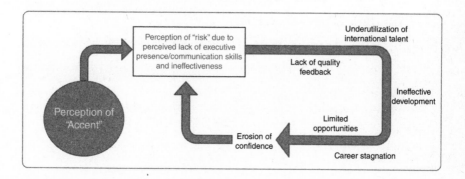

Organizational Analysis

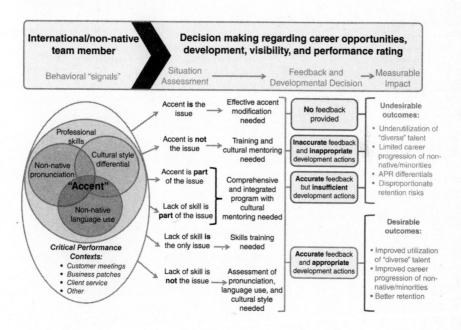

Breaking Down the Accent Cycle

Breaking the "accent" cycle:
Points of breakdown and solution

Breakdown point	Solution
① Inadequate or inaccurate situation assessment	A comprehensive assessment process that factors pronunciation, language use, and culture across critical performance contexts is needed.
② Feedback either **_not_** provided or ineffective	The skill of providing constructive feedback with development plans needs to be expected and developed as a managerial skill.
③ Insufficient/ineffective development solutions used or selected	The current development options need to be audited for quality and comprehensiveness (additional solutions may need to be developed/ added, depending on results), and solutions need to be aligned with improved assessments.
④ Insufficient attention/skill to set expectations and position/ credentialize diverse talent with clients	Development opportunities need to include managerial/leadership skills development for positioning and credentializing diverse talent and non-native team members with clients.

Debunk Your Beliefs

CONFIDENCE

POPULAR BELIEF

I lack confidence because my skills in English are not great.

Some possible results of my belief:
• I demonstrate mediocre communication skills.
• My voice is underdeveloped.
• I might not be chosen to face clients.
• I may not get a promotion.

CONFIDENCE

PUT THE BELIEF TO THE TEST

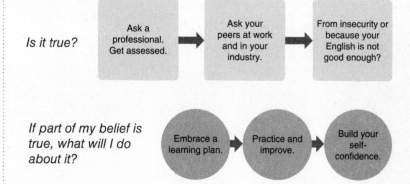

Is it true?

| Ask a professional. Get assessed. | Ask your peers at work and in your industry. | From insecurity or because your English is not good enough? |

If part of my belief is true, what will I do about it?

Embrace a learning plan. → Practice and improve. → Build your self-confidence.

UNDERSTATE ABILITIES

MY BELIEF

It is polite to tell people my English is not so good. After all, I am a non-native speaker and do not wish to appear arrogant. I do, however, communicate well in English.

Some possible results of underestimating my English:
- Others think my English is not capable.
- I am being chosen to take language classes.
- I am not assertive.

UNDERSTATE ABILITIES

PUT THE BELIEF TO THE TEST

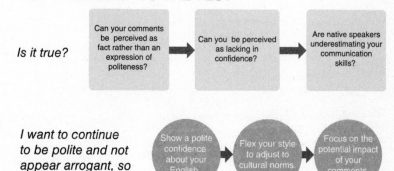

Is it true?

Can your comments be perceived as fact rather than an expression of politeness? → Can you be perceived as lacking in confidence? → Are native speakers underestimating your communication skills?

I want to continue to be polite and not appear arrogant, so what can I do?

Show a polite confidence about your English. → Flex your style to adjust to cultural norms. → Focus on the potential impact of your comments.

ENGLISH UNDER A MICROSCOPE

POPULAR BELIEF

My language is constantly being evaluated by native-speaking managers and colleagues. I'm under pressure to "get it right." I should avoid mistakes and use safe language.

Some results of my belief:
• I hesitate in critical situations. I am cautious about my contributions.
• My capacity for expressive English gets locked.
• My core principles and full potential are hidden as a result of safe English.
• I avoid essential business interactions, so I don't lose face by making mistakes.

ENGLISH UNDER A MICROSCOPE

PUT THE BELIEF TO THE TEST

Is it true?

| Who is really inspecting? Your organization? Your boss? Your peers? | → | Get the opinion of an influencer, a role model, and other international professionals. | → | Examine your findings and reevaluate your beliefs. |

What will I do about it?

| Seek the help of diversity and inclusion professionals | → | Believe that your ideas are more important than the English that you use. | → | Practice delivering messages with more confidence. | → | Show those around you that you can deliver messages with impact. |

ACCENT

POPULAR BELIEF

My accent is too thick.
I should slow down so people can understand me.

Some possible results of my belief:
• I try to speak slowly, hoping to be understood.
• I have given up and speak quickly because no one understands me anyway.
• Management believes my English is not effective.

ACCENT

PUT THE BELIEF TO THE TEST

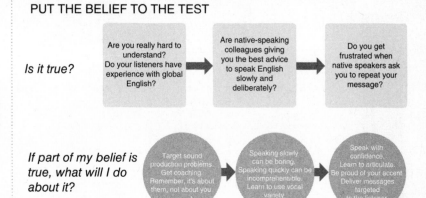

Is it true?

| Are you really hard to understand? Do your listeners have experience with global English? | → | Are native-speaking colleagues giving you the best advice to speak English slowly and deliberately? | → | Do you get frustrated when native speakers ask you to repeat your message? |

If part of my belief is true, what will I do about it?

| Target sound production problems. Get coaching. Remember, it's about them, not about you. | → | Speaking slowly can be boring. Speaking quickly can be incomprehensible. Learn to use vocal variety. | → | Speak with confidence. Learn to articulate. Be proud of your accent. Deliver messages targeted to the listener. |

Recovery Skills

RECOVERY SKILLS

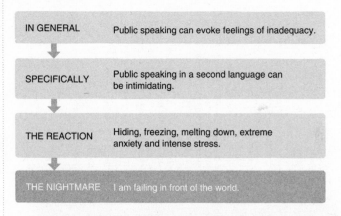

| IN GENERAL | Public speaking can evoke feelings of inadequacy. |

| SPECIFICALLY | Public speaking in a second language can be intimidating. |

| THE REACTION | Hiding, freezing, melting down, extreme anxiety and intense stress. |

| THE NIGHTMARE | I am failing in front of the world. |

RECOVERY SKILLS

TRIGGERS	ACTUAL FEARS	ADDED FEARS FOR NON-NATIVE SPEAKERS
I lose my place. My mind goes blank.	I panic...	By losing my place, I am afraid I will lose my ability to speak in free-flow English.
Can't think of a word/phrase	They think I am overly nervous and cannot control the moment.	They think my English is poor.
Don't know the answer	I am losing credibility.	They think I lack intelligence.
Being challenged	I feel threatened and uncertain how to respond.	My English deteriorates under stress.
Nonparticipation	The audience is rejecting me and my content.	I don't have the language capacity to engage them.

HOW TO RECOVER

TRIGGER	TECHNIQUES
My mind goes blank.	Be calm. Find word or phrase yourself. Ask the audience for help. Smile, it happens to everyone. Breathe, recover, and continue.
I can't find the correct word.	Stop looking for it. Train yourself to find other words, structures. Trust that you can think in English on your feet. Train yourself through practice with peers. Stop translating.
I don't know the answer to a pertinent question.	Look at it as an opportunity to follow up. Tell the group that you will get back to them. When you do, you will regain and enhance your credibility. Many people do not follow up. If someone else knows the answer, use that person as a resource. If not, park the question and follow up. If it is a serious omission, apologize and then follow up. Move on.
Someone is challenging my content.	Welcome pushback. It helps sharpen the discussion. Ask the person to elaborate, and then open to the audience for discussion. Show respect and acceptance that this person is engaged. Show fortitude when the pushback is severe. Never let them see you sweat. Be open, honest, sincere.
Someone is challenging me.	Remain professional at all times and try to take the conversation off line.
My audience does not participate.	Learn effective facilitator skills, and engage the audience through guided activities.

Vocabulary Learning System: Vocabulary Log

Of the two types of vocabulary—active and passive—humans naturally have a much larger passive vocabulary. Accordingly, the best method of increasing your everyday terminology is to transfer words that you understand but rarely use. You need to actively retrieve these words from your passive reservoir and begin using them.

Objective: To increase your active vocabulary by 50 to 75 words per year.

Assignment: Get a spiral notebook. Aim to explore one new word family per week.

Process: Words are everywhere. You hear them, read them, see them, and know them.

Identify a word in context. For example, you see the following sentence and can identify the word *flaw*.

"The design had a flaw."

Get to Know the Family

1. Create a "web" in your vocabulary log: one word per page.
2. Identify other parts of speech and uses of the word *flaw*, such as flawed, flawless, flawlessly, and so on.
   a. Google the word *flaw* to get a better feel for the word.
   b. Find synonyms and antonyms, and add them to your notebook.
   c. Make a point to use the word during your normal oral/written communication at least twice that week.
   d. Make a point to use a different part of speech from the family in your normal oral/written communication at least twice that week.
   e. Earmark the page in your log or fold it in half; you own it—case closed!

3. Revisit the closed pages occasionally to make sure you still own them.

As you can see, learning new vocabulary comes with a bit of work. The result, however, will have huge benefits.

Framing an Idea

The concept is to speak at a normal or fast pace, and then slow down when you get to the particular idea that you want the audience to remember. In essence, you frame the idea you want the audience to remember the most.

Example One (at a normal to quick pace)   The purpose of the meeting today is to go over the (slow down pace and announce) incredible results (quicken the pace again) that we discovered in this year's survey.

Example Two (at a normal to quick pace)   The company is about to announce the fourth-quarter results (slow down pace and announce), which we all hope (quicken the pace again) will show a significant profit.

Framing an Idea: Exercises

Record your favorite newscaster and replay how he or she frames an idea. Also, pay attention to the vocal variety the newscaster uses:

- The rising and falling of the intonation
- The changing rate of speech
- The fluctuations in the volume

Rewind the recording, pause it, and practice along with the newscaster. You are now studying the way a professional delivers messages.

Volume 1, 2, 3 Exercise Scale

Find Your Presentation Voice

Purpose

To understand what volume works best for you.

Agenda

- Bring a colleague or two to your company's largest conference room.
- Have them sit in the back.
- You stand in the front.

Exercises

1. Say the number "one" at the volume level that you use in conversation. Ask them if they can hear you comfortably. Is it too low?
2. Say the number "two" but double your volume this time. Again, ask them if they can hear you comfortably. Is it too low or too loud?
3. Say the number "three" and double your volume again. Again, ask them if they can hear you comfortably. Is it too low or too loud?

Based on their answers, you should discover what level works for you when presenting. Don't be surprised if you feel like you are shouting at levels 2 or 3 but your colleagues tell you that is your appropriate volume. When presenting, you will have to come out of your comfort zone. Practice several times.

Verbal Dexterity Exercise

Purpose

To become more proficient in speaking clearly using vocal variety.

Agenda

- Find a private room.
- Use your smartphone to audio record yourself.
- Choose some content to read aloud: Internet, magazine, or other.

Exercise: Part 1   Audio record yourself reading the passage aloud. Read for the sole purpose of being understood—as clearly as possible. (The exercise works best if you can have a colleague listen and provide a summary back to you.)

Exercise: Part 2   Audio record yourself again reading the same passage. This time, pretend that you are the anchor on the six o'clock news. There are two million people listening. Read the passage with great enthusiasm. Frame ideas. Add passion through your intonation.

Exercise: Part 3   Compare the two recordings.

Notes

Chapter 1: It Takes Two to Tango

1. www.tangoconcepts.com/blog/2008/02/tango-not-difficult-but
   -not-easy.html.
2. Mark Robson, Foreword to *The English Effect: The Impact of English, What It's Worth to the UK and Why It Matters to the World* (London: British Council, 2013), D096.
3. Carla Power, "Not the Queen's English: Non-Native English Speakers Now Outnumber Native Ones 3 to 1," *Newsweek* (International Ed.), March 7, 2005, 46.
4. Miriam Jordan, "Limited English Limits Job Prospects: Study Finds 1 in 10 Working-Age Adults Has Limited Proficiency," *Wall Street Journal*, September 24, 2014.
5. www.tangoconcepts.com/blog/tangoscene.html.
6. http://blog.usa.skanska.com/why-its-time-to-have-a-conversation
   -about-workplace-inclusion/.

Chapter 2: Speaking Clearly

1. Steve Maraboli, *Life, the Truth, and Being Free* (Port Washington, NY: A Better Today Publishing, 2009).
2. Claude M. Steele, Steven J. Spencer, and Joshua Aronson, "Contending with Group Image: The Psychology of Stereotype and

Social Identity Threat," in *Advances in Experimental Social Psychology*, vol. 34, ed. Mark P. Zanna (Amsterdam: Academic Press), 379–440.

3. Henry Kissinger interview on Charlie Rose (1992), https://www.youtube.com/watch?v=2Cnm8aKA2fU.

4. Agata Gluszek and John F. Dovidio, "Speaking with a Nonnative Accent: Perceptions of Bias, Communication Difficulties, and Belonging in the United States," *Journal of Language and Social Psychology* 29 (June 2010).

5. Dennis Preston, "The Uses of Folk Linguistics," *International Journal of Applied Linguistics* 3, no. 2 (April 2007): 181–259.

6. G. Demby, *CODE SWITCH: Race and Identity, Remix*. NPR, April 8, 2013, www.npr.org/sections/codeswitch/2013/04/08/176064688/how-code-switching-explains-the-world.

7. A. G. Greenwald and M. R. Banaji, "Implicit Social Cognition: Attitudes, Self-Esteem, and Stereotypes," *Psychological Review* 102 (1995): 4–27.

8. S. L. A. Heblich, "The Effect of Perceived Regional Accents on Individual Economic Behavior: A Lab Experiment on Linguistic Performance, Cognitive Ratings and Economic Decisions," *PLoS ONE* 10, no. 2 (February 2015): e0113475. Erratum in *PLoS ONE* 10, no. 5 (2015): e0124732.

9. A. L. Souza, K. Byers-Heinlein, and D. Poulin-Dubois, "Bilingual and Monolingual Children Prefer Native-Accented Speakers," *Frontiers in Psychology* 4 (2013): 953.

10. L. F. Huang, "Political Skill: Explaining the Effects of Nonnative Accent on Managerial Hiring and Entrepreneurial Investment Decisions," *Journal of Applied Psychology* 98, no. 6 (2013): 1005–1017.

Chapter 3: Speaking with Impact

1. *Rush Hour* (film), 1998, New Line Cinema, distributed in United States and China.

2. Susan Cain, *Quiet: The Power of Introverts in a World That Can't Stop Talking* (New York: Crown, 2012).

3. *A Beautiful Mind* (film), Universal Pictures, Dreamlike Pictures, December 2001.

Chapter 4: Developing a Compelling Narrative

1. Bruce Springsteen made this statement as part of his induction speech of the E Street Band into the Rock & Roll Hall of Fame (www.stoneponylondon.net/rrhofresb.htm).

2. There are, of course, many definitions of leadership. Ours is anchored in the works of Bass and Hollander, who emphasized it as a process of influence within a group, rather than locating it in positional attributes or mere personal characteristics. According to Hollander, "Leadership is a process of influence between a leader and those who are followers" (Edwin P. Hollander, *Leadership Dynamics: A Practical Guide to Effective Relationships*, New York: Free Press, 1978). Bass describes leadership as "an interaction between two or more members of a group that often involves a structuring or restructuring of the situation and the perceptions and expectations of members. . . . Leadership occurs when one group member modifies the motivation or competencies of others in the group" (Bernard M. Bass, *Bass & Stogdill's Handbook of Leadership: Theory, Research, and Managerial Applications*, 3rd ed., New York: Free Press, 1990, 19–20).

3. See www.gamesindustry.biz/articles/2015–04–22-gaming-will -hit-usd91–5-billion-this-year-newzoo.

4. Rüdiger Wischenbart, "The Business of Books," Frankfurter Buchmesse/Frankfurt Book Fair, 2015.

5. Paul J. Zak, "Why Your Brain Loves Good Storytelling," *Harvard Business Review*, October 28, 2014, https://hbr.org/2014/10/ why-your-brain-loves-good-storytelling.

6. Neurobiologist Paul Zak has demonstrated that stories are linked to the production of the neurochemical oxytocin. Oxytocin levels increase when we experience kindness and trust, and is

essential to the motivation to cooperate, which in turn increases oxytocin levels in others.

7. Zak, "Why Your Brain Loves Good Storytelling."

8. Joseph Campbell, *The Hero with a Thousand Faces* (Princeton, NJ: Princeton University Press, 1949), 23.

9. According to Basic Knowledge 101 (www.basicknowledge101 .com/index.html), the average human brain contains approximately 400 miles of capillaries, as well as 86 billion microscopic neurons that stand in constant synaptic communication with one another, averaging an estimated 10 quadrillion calculations per second. With more than 500 trillion neural connections, our brain performs a complex array of mental processes that generate and regulate our sensations and perceptions, how we reason, our emotions, mental imagery, attention span, memory, and learning.

10. https://www.statista.com/topics/1293/market-research/ and https://www.emarketer.com/Article/Advertisers-Will-Spend -Nearly-600-Billion-Worldwide-2015/1011691.

11. https://www.linkdex.com/en-us/inked/brand-story-examples/.

12. See World Economic Forum report: "Shaping the Future of Construction: A Breakthrough in Mindset and Technology," May 2016.

13. See *Breaking the Bamboo Ceiling: Career Strategies for Asians* by Jane Hyun (New York: HarperCollins, 2005).

14. R. J. House, P. J. Hanges, M. Javidan, P. Dorfman, and V. Gupta, *Culture, Leadership, and Organizations: The GLOBE Study of 62 Societies* (Thousand Oaks, CA: Sage Publications, 2004).

15. Sylvia Ann Hewlett, Lauren Leader-Chivée, Laura Sherbin, and Joanne Gordon with Fabiola Dieudonné, *Executive Presence* (Center for Talent Innovation, 2012).

16. See The Conference Board, CEO Challenge 2016. https://www .conference-board.org/ceo-challenge2016/.

About the Authors

D. Vincent Varallo is cofounder and CEO of Lead in English, a firm specializing in talent development solutions for international professionals working in English. He and his team have helped thousands of international professionals become more adept communicators. Vince also founded Varallo International in 1995, which serves Fortune 500 companies in public speaking, business writing, and intercultural-communication skills. He coaches global executives around the world.

Joerg Schmitz is cofounder and Managing Partner at ThomasLeland. He is a business anthropologist with extensive experience helping leaders and organizations navigate the challenges and opportunities of culture and globalization. As a senior advisor and consultant, he has developed innovative approaches to intercultural management, diversity and inclusiveness, global talent and team optimization, and leadership development. He develops cultural transformation strategies for clients worldwide.

Stephan M. Mardyks is a world-renowned expert in the field of global learning and development. He has created and engineered countless highly acclaimed learning architectures for top programs across the world. Stephan is the CEO of SMCOV and cofounder of Wisdom Destinations, TrapTales, and Streamline Certified. He is also Managing Partner at Lead in English and ThomasLeland. His past experiences include serving as Co-COO at FranklinCovey.

For more information about *Lead in English*, please visit its website at www.leadinenglish.com/.

Index